The Tonbridge

in the footsteps of m ...ights

by Deborah Cole

Printed by Berforts Information Press Limited 2013

Preface

Tonbridge has a long distance circular walk seven centuries old. A record of this 'perambulation of the lowy (castle lands) of Tonbridge' has lain virtually undisturbed on a single sheet of parchment in Canterbury Cathedral since 1279. The walk was not for leisure, but a jury of 24 local lords and knights set out to determine what lands belonged to the Earl, Gilbert of Tonbridge Castle and what to the Archbishop of Canterbury and others. The Archbishop's copy in Canterbury Cathedral is in mediaeval Latin and was translated by John Harris in 1719 (The History of Kent in 5 parts, Vol. 1, p. 320). 80 years later Edward Hasted refused to include it in his great work on the history of Kent, because 'the places as well as the names of persons mentioned in these perambulations being obsolete and now totally unknown, the insertion of them in this place can give so little information to the reader' (History and Topographical Survey of Kent 2nd ed., Vol. V, p.175). Since that time the perambulation route has been largely forgotten apart from V.W. Dumbreck's referrals to parts of it in his article, 'The Lowy of Tonbridge,' Archaeologia Cantiana, 1958, Vol. lxxii.

Not being deterred and knowing that you must never believe all you read, I set about transcribing and translating it from the mediaeval Latin to check spellings and possible omissions. Knowing that 13th century documents do not come thick and fast in Tonbridge we need to make the most of what there is. On the perambulation, 59 places were visited. Of these, I discovered that 17 still exist. If other places are added which are recorded in early histories, documents and old maps, then another 17 can be located with reasonable confidence, making more than half in total. I joined up the 34 places on a map and discovered as Dumbreck did, that the jury appeared to follow old parish boundaries but not exclusively.

I drew a map of the route and then walked it in stages to see if the landscape revealed any clues that might identify missing places such as ponds, old roads, house names etc. Public footpaths were found on or near the route and the walking began in the sunny month of March 2012.

I made many discoveries on the way; missing places identified by associated features and old names seen on houses and roads. That was exciting enough, but to top it all, I found the countryside around Tonbridge remarkably varied and beautiful, with often unexpected but glorious views. It had to be shared and so a natural next step was to link up the footpaths to make a long distance walk around Tonbridge....in the footsteps of mediaeval knights. Places and features of historic interest of all periods can be seen on the route, and some were familiar to the knights. They would have stopped occasionally to rest and the good news is that on every walk there is a pub, cafe or shop so that like them you can rest and refresh and perhaps speculate on how much has changed in the seven centuries since they made their journey.

DC
Tonbridge, July 2013

Acknowledgements

I would like to thank Kent Archaeological Society for an award from the Allen Grove Fund enabling me to publish. Members of Tonbridge and Leigh Historical Societies offered advice and tested walks. Friends and family have accompanied me on walks to test directions and especially Shelley Phillips with dog, Lily. My family also helped with proof reading and my daughter Cathy created the pencil illustrations. The photographs were taken by the author. Two images of the priory were inserted from www.tonbridgehistory.org.uk (7.002, 7.003; © Tonbridge Historical Society 2011) with the permission of the society. Three images were taken from internet sources which are now in the public domain such as Turner's *Pembury Mill*, Landseer's *Monarch of the Glen* and the illustration from *Foxe's Book of Martyrs*. The image of Gilbert 'the Red' is of a stained glass window at Tewkesbury Abbey and is included with permission ©Vicar and Churchwardens of Tewkesbury Abbey. Printed historical works were consulted and they are acknowledged in the preface. Others I would like to name here are K. P. Witney 1976, 'The Jutish Forest.' This exhaustive work on the manorial system of Kent was useful for place name interpretation and locations. Another very useful source was J. Cunningham ed., 2007 'An Historical Atlas of Tunbridge Wells,' Royal Tunbridge Wells Civic Society, Local History Monograph No 7.

Contents

Introduction   7

The Walk in 12 stages:

1 Shipbourne to Stallions Green   15
2 Stallions Green to Barnes Street   19
3 Barnes Street to Five Oak Green   26
4 Five Oak Green to Old Pembury   30
5 Old Pembury to Pembury Green   34
6 Pembury Green to Tunbridge Wells   38
7 Tunbridge Wells to Stockland Green   44
8 Stockland Green to Penshurst   49
9 Penshurst to Chiddingstone Causeway   55
10 Chiddingstone Causeway to Nizels   60
11 Nizels to Underriver   65
12 Underriver to Shipbourne   70

Link Walks:

1 Tonbridge to Ford Green Bridge   75
2 Tonbridge to Penshurst   81

Circular Walks:

1 Shipbourne and the Bourne Valley   86
2 Hadlow and the Common   91
3 Hadlow and Golden Green   96
4 Golden Green and Five Oak Green   102
5 Five Oak Green and Capel   109
6 Old Pembury and Romford   115
7 Pembury Green and the Pantiles   122
8 Tunbridge Wells and Rusthall   129
9 Speldhurst and Poundsbridge   136
10 Penshurst and the Medway Valley   142
11 Penshurst and the Eden Valley   147
12 Chiddingstone and Coppings   154
13 Weald and Fletchers Green   160
14 Weald and Underriver   164
15 Underriver and Shipbourne   171

(handwritten annotations, right column)

Distance
5 miles
3 miles
4·5 miles
5 miles
5 miles
5·5 miles
7·5 miles
6 miles
4·5 miles
3·5 miles
5·5 miles
Avg 5 miles
2·5 miles
6·5 miles
5·5 miles

5

Key to Maps

A B start and end of perambulation on circular walks

――― road

START walk starts here

∿ stream

- - -→- - route with direction arrow

- - -S - - - with stile

- - - FB- - with footbridge

• • • • • • • 19th century parish boundary

pub or cafe nearby

mediaeval mill

The maps were drawn from OS 1:25000 Explorer Maps with permission granted.

Introduction

In 1279 Gilbert Clare, 'the Red' of Tonbridge Castle whose full title was the 9th Earl of Clare (Suffolk), 6th Earl of Hertford, 7th Earl of Gloucester and Lord of Glamorgan was 36 years old and the Clare family were at the height of their power and wealth. Just five years earlier, Gilbert had entertained the new King Edward I and his Queen, Eleanor, in Tonbridge Castle which was newly built and extended in stone. He had just built Caerphilly Castle, thought to be partly modelled on Tonbridge.

Residing in a new and grander castle, often joining military campaigns and needing a lifestyle to match the royal court, Gilbert was in need of revenue. With the help of his bailiff he had to ensure that his lands around Tonbridge known as 'the lowy' of Tonbridge were as profitable as they could be and could supply the castle.

The Norman Conquest and the Lowy of Tonbridge

The origin of the word 'lowy' is lost in history but is thought to be derived from an old French (Gallic) word which gives us the more modern 'league;' a measure of land that can be walked in an hour or so. The distance was variable and in the case of Tonbridge Castle it seemed to include all land within 4 to 5 miles of the castle. There are echoes here, of good King Wenceslas 'a good league hence...right against the forest fence.'

The lowy was either granted to the first Clare, Richard Fitzgilbert by William the Conqueror after the battle of Hastings or Richard himself took possession of it. It was important for William to have the main route from London to Normandy via Winchelsea and Hastings defended at the Medway crossing and Richard probably thought of it as fair reward for his support in the conquest of England.

Richard of Tonbridge (as he became known) built his castle soon after 1066 and the lowy was to provide for its upkeep, providing rental as well as produce from the demesne land of forests, rivers and farms. The arrival of the Normans, the building of the first castle with its huge earthwork and appropriation of land must have astonished and dismayed the local people.

From Domesday Book it is clear that the lowy included land attached to 24 different manors so it was already accounted for before the Conquest and in fact was largely owned by the Archbishop of Canterbury. The entries under each manor usually read; 'Richard of Tonbridge has in his territory.....'

Post Conquest

In the confusion of the Conquest it is easy to see how lands could be snapped up and grants awarded at random by King William where he thought this was necessary for defence. Previous ownership would not necessarily be considered. Virtually all of the 'lowy' had belonged to the Archbishop of Canterbury and part to the Bishop of Rochester and others, but it was a long way from Canterbury. Nevertheless, from the 11th century the church authorities were active in trying to recover the lands taken from them. Not only were church lands taken but the lowy cut a swath through the Saxon administration based on the county divisions of the 'hundreds' each of which had their own court.

1279 Perambulation of the Lowy

Gilbert and his bailiff tried raising money and supplies from the lowy without knowing the exact boundary (or they conveniently forgot). The perambulation or walk to determine the boundary in 1279 became necessary as a result of many years of disputes between the Earls of Gloucester (as the Clares had become) and the Archbishop and others. A jury of 24 lords and knights (12 chosen by the Archbishop and 12 by the Earl) walked the boundary, probably with horses, so that hedges and streams could be crossed and the distance covered more quickly. A local knight and justice, Lord Stephen of Penshurst presided at the castle.

Finding the Route

The original perambulation (Archbishop's copy, written in mediaeval Latin) can be viewed in Canterbury Cathedral Archives Library. It mentions a number of places that can be identified today. By linking them and looking at the course of old parish and 'hundred' boundaries (pre 1871) it was possible to piece together the most probable route.

This route was walked as nearly as possible along public footpaths to identify places such as hills, ponds, fields, and other details not easily seen on a map. Some footpaths follow the lowy boundary and when it was finally mapped, the shape of it was found to be almost circular and defined an area around the castle of 4 to 5 miles in all directions (see page 12).

A 13th Century Tonbridge Circular Walk

There are public footpaths sufficiently close to the 13th century perambulation that can be linked and made into a long distance circular walk of 33 miles. Starting in Shipbourne the walk goes through or near Hadlow, Golden Green, Five Oak Green, Pembury, Tunbridge Wells, Speldhurst, Penshurst, Chiddingstone Causeway, Sevenoaks Weald, and Underriver before ending back in Shipbourne.

The countryside around Tonbridge is extraordinarily beautiful and dramatic changes are seen from one part of the route to another. There are challenging steep hills and deep valleys, gentle rolling pastures, romantic bluebell woods, apple orchards, tinkling brooks, wide floodplains, huge skies and glorious views.

Even though the best of the Tonbridge countryside is explored here, you are never far from picturesque local villages with their shops, pubs, cafes and fascinating history.

The walk is easily divided into shorter sections and some points on the route are accessible by public transport. Penshurst (Chiddingstone Causeway) and Tunbridge Wells Railway Stations are close to the route. Buses (Arriva) can be taken from Tonbridge to Hadlow, Golden Green, Five Oak Green, Pembury, Tunbridge Wells and Sevenoaks Weald. More details are given at the head of each walk.

Information about accommodation and camping sites can be found at the Tonbridge Tourist Information Office at Tonbridge Castle.

Two 25 mile Walks from the Castle

Tonbridge Castle is the centre of the lowy and a good place to start a 25 mile walk round the northern or southern half of the perambulation using the Medway as a link (west to Penshurst and east to Ford Green Bridge). The link walks are pleasant walks in themselves and there is a good circular walk between Tonbridge and Ford Green Bridge, returning through the Clares' former deer park of Postern. Directions for the link walks are included in this book.

Fifteen 2 - 8 mile Circular Walks

Short circular walks, starting in villages with public transport and/or parking complete the book. They each include a section of the perambulation plus yet more beautiful countryside and interesting history. They all pass at least one pub/cafe/shop.

The following symbols indicate the type of walk in the book:

Perambulation
12 sections

2 Link Walks
East/West

15 Circular
Walks

A 13th Century Walk Around Tonbridge

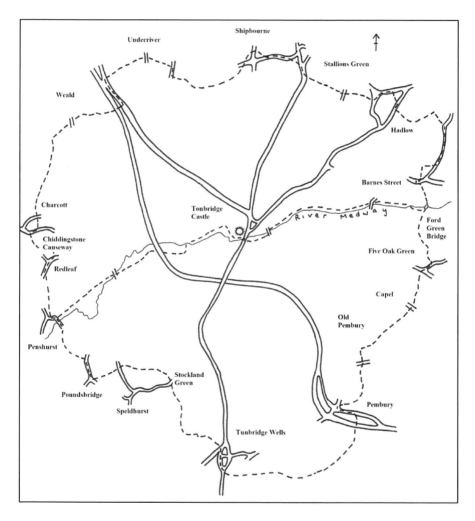

© Crown copyright 2013 Ordnance Survey 100054134

Geology and Relief of Tonbridge Area

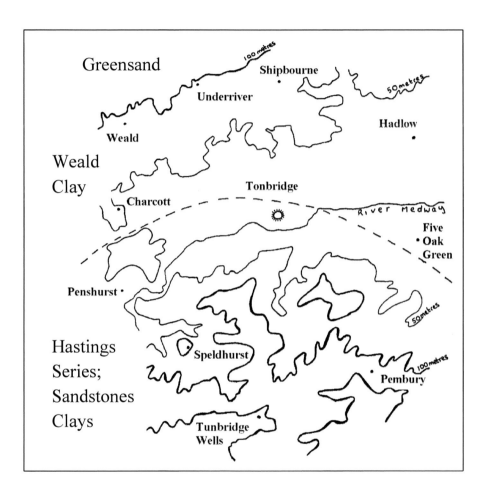

© Crown copyright 2013 Ordnance Survey 100054134

Walk Notes

- This book is arranged so that the perambulation is described in 12 stages, followed by 2 link walks to and from Tonbridge Castle and then 15 circular walks on and around the route.

> *I, Sir Stephen of Penshurst presided over the perambulation which was presented to me by the Jury at Tonbridge Castle. Each walk begins with a relevant quotation from the document.*

- Directions on the perambulation route are coloured green; walks off route in yellow. *In among the directions are historical notes of interest, given in italics.* If you notice any changes to the routes or any mistakes then please advise by emailing: info@tonbridgecircularwalk.co.uk

- There is a simple sketch map at the end of each walk. It is recommended that you also take the relevant O.S. map, indicated at the head of each walk.

- Most walks involve going over stiles and the number of stiles is indicated at the head of each walk.

- A feature of wealden walks in wet weather is sticky clay and all have muddy sections. The walks are best enjoyed after dry weather but take appropriate footwear as some parts seem to be permanently muddy.

- All walks involve at least one road section sometimes without pavements. Be aware of traffic; cyclists as well as cars.

- Be aware of livestock, especially if taking dogs and close gates if they were already closed.

Happy Walking!

Shipbourne to Stallions Green

Maps:	OS Explorer 147, 148
Distance:	2 miles (mile 0)
Stiles:	none
Start:	The Chaser Inn; TQ 593523
Parking:	Shipbourne Green
Refresh:	The Chaser Inn, Shipbourne

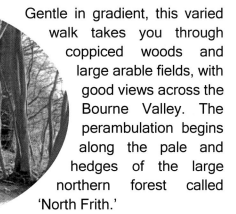

Gentle in gradient, this varied walk takes you through coppiced woods and large arable fields, with good views across the Bourne Valley. The perambulation begins along the pale and hedges of the large northern forest called 'North Frith.'

'The jury..began the lowy at Somegate..in the parish of Tonbridge and so along the hedges and pale including the northern forest to Claygate and so to Larkhale, therefore the said forest and Larkhale be within the lowy..'

15

'Somegate' no longer exists but is near Shipbourne, so from Shipbourne to Claygate the perambulation route is followed closely. Soon after Claygate you will follow the course of the forest pale along a high boundary bank through woods on the edge of the North Frith, as the jurors did.

Start at The Chaser Inn and cross the road (Stumble Hill) to the Common so that you are on the same side of the road as the red telephone box. In between the first two trees, look for a grassy footpath (not signed but marked on the OS Map) that bears left across the Common. Go along the path passing right of a large oak tree and towards a line of trees. Keep the trees on your right for a while and arrive at a path junction. Look out right, for a gate set back in the trees. Go through it and cross a field to Back Lane. Turn left along the lane and then right along Reeds Lane.

The Tonbridge 'North Frith' forest rose uphill on the right as it does today but probably extended further north towards the lanes.

Pass 'Martins' on the right and then turn right along a byway until you reach a lane. Turn right here to Claygate.

Claygate was an entrance in the forest pale of the North Frith. On an ancient road; it was used by Wrotham folk (long before the Normans) for access to the forest and the Medway Valley.

At the T junction, turn right along Puttenden Road and continue across a bridge over the Bourne and uphill passing houses on your left. Just beyond 'Hookwood' (the third house) turn left through woods at a footpath sign. Continue to a way-marked path junction.

16

Note the boundary stone on the left. From here Hadlow Parish is on your right and West Peckham on your left.

Go directly ahead and continue along the top of the boundary bank.

This bank is probably the line of the forest pale and the perambulation route. Hadlow and North Frith were part of the lowy of Tonbridge. On the West Peckham side, Clearhedges was disputed land. The Clares had tried to take it unsuccessfully.

Continue along the bank until you arrive at a junction with a broad track. Turn right and almost immediately left following footpath signs. Descend through the wood and eventually turn right into a field, then continue alongside the edge of the wood and then a hedge. Pass into the next field through a gap and continue towards a belt of trees ahead. Turn right just before and continue with the trees on your left until you emerge on High House Lane at Stallions Green. Turn left, pass a bungalow and soon reach a footpath sign on the right side of the road.

Larkhale is in the Stallions Green area but probably further north along High House Lane where the Hadlow Parish boundary follows the lane.

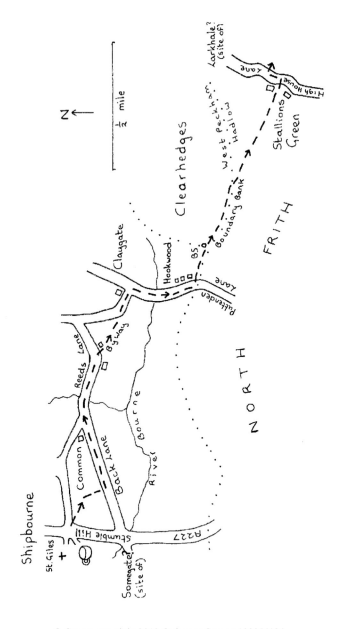

2

Stallions Green to Barnes Street

Maps:	OS Explorer 136, 148
Distance:	4 miles (mile 2)
Stiles:	4 stiles
Start:	High House Lane; TQ 622508
Parking:	Stallions Green (narrow road)
Refresh:	The Harrow, Hadlow;
	The Bell, Golden Green

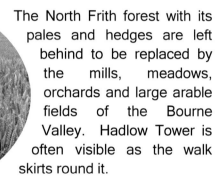

The North Frith forest with its pales and hedges are left behind to be replaced by the mills, meadows, orchards and large arable fields of the Bourne Valley. Hadlow Tower is often visible as the walk skirts round it.

'..from Larkhale...through the midst of Lomewood to..the domus of Peter Fromund..to the Kings Highway which includes the land of Hugo de Waldis and..to the messuage of Pepin and so directly over the field to the hall of Peter de la Mare...'

The perambulation lists tenants whose lands or houses it passes near. A third of all properties in the perambulation are in this four mile section.

The Hadlow boundary zigzags wildly in now empty fields, but in the 13th century it must have skirted round and sometimes through individual tenements.

Start

Start on High House Lane at Stallions Green with the bungalow on your left. Take the next footpath on the right, go over the stile and follow the right hedge to the river Bourne. Cross a footbridge, go across a meadow and through the next hedge. Over to the right marked by a clump of trees is the site of a mediaeval moat. Continue towards the left side of the moat.

The story of this moat site is not known although there was probably a house here in the 13th century. Moats were commonly dug around wealthier houses in the 13th and 14th centuries. A spring by the house higher up the hill supplied the moat house and in time the moat was probably abandoned in favour of the higher site.

From the moat corner continue in the same direction uphill, across a large field. Hadlow Tower will appear ahead. At the field corner, go through a kissing gate to the road (Carpenters Lane) at Steers Place.

There is a road sign here to The Common. It was called Hadlow Common and before that Lomewood as in the perambulation. There is still a street in Hadlow called Lomewood Way.

Cross Carpenters Lane and continue along Steers Place in the direction of the Common. Reach a T junction with Common Road and turn right.

The Common 'Lomewood' was on both sides of the road, so that as the jurors did in 1279 you are walking through the 'midst of Lomewood.'

Continue past Laxton Farm on your left and when you reach footpath signs, turn right along an enclosed path and come out on a road. Turn left and continue to Maidstone Road (A26). Turn right and continue along the pavement to Cemetery Lane on your left, just before the 'The Harrow' Inn.

Close to this junction there was once a cross called Durrants Cross offering protection for travellers walking from the village of Hadlow as they left the safety of their houses and entered Lomewood.

More than once the cemetery on Cemetery Lane was thought to be a good site for burials as two Romano/British cremations (2,000 years old) were discovered there in the late 19th Century.

The late W.V. Dumbreck is buried there. An eminent Hadlow historian, in 1958 he translated and published part of the 1279 perambulation document in 'Archaeologia Cantiana'. It was an important source for this project.

Continue on the Maidstone Road past 'The Harrow' to some cottages. After the last cottage turn left along a footpath signed East Peckham.

On the right at the entrance to the footpath, there is a narrow stretch of water which is in fact, a stream that used to flow down from the Common and sometimes flood Hadlow.

Follow the enclosed path to a field, continue across to the next hedge and cross a footbridge. Go across the next field and then zigzag with the path around hedges on your left, looking for a well hidden left turn through a straight section of hedge. Once through the hedge there is an orchard on the left and a high silver birch hedge on the right. Turn right and go round the hedge and continue alongside it with a smaller hedge on your right. Continue through the next field to a kissing gate ahead in a high hedge. Go through to Cemetery Lane, turn left and then immediately right into Goblands Farm entrance (a small industrial estate).

Go forward and take the next left towards a black painted clapboard building. Turn right along the track passing buildings on your right. At the end go left and then right after a small group of painted containers. Follow a grassy track straight ahead between fields and about 100 metres short of the wood, bear left across the field and continue through the wood.

This wood is on the parish boundary and the jurors probably came here where there was a cluster of tenements. Some of the fields were called 'boundsfields' in the 19th century and a part belonged to the Fromund family in the mediaeval period; perhaps Peter's house was here.

The 'beating of the bounds' which used to take place during Rogationtide in May, zigzagged round fields and crossed over stiles. One such stile was known as 'the cider stile' where the Goding family (later the Golding family of Golding Hop fame) offered the bound beaters a pail of cider.

Come out of the wood to a path junction, turn right and then bear left across a large field towards another wood. At the end of the field, turn right and then immediately right through the same field on another trajectory. Cross a stile into a sports ground and go across towards two wooden posts marking a gap in the hedge. Go through and come to Bells Farm Lane. Turn right.

There is reason to think that this road is the 'Kings Highway' of the perambulation since the parish boundary follows the road and therefore it is likely the road is as old. There are very few places around Tonbridge where roads are aligned with parish boundaries.

Continue along the lane and pass Bells Farmhouse on your left. Shortly join Court Lane coming in from the right and keep directly ahead. Soon you will come to a three way junction at Kent House Farm.

The 'Kings Highway' is said in the perambulation to include the lands of Hugo de Waldis (Weald). The suggestion is that while his lands were within, his house was without. The name Kent House Farm is interesting because there are other Kent Farms or Kent Houses on the boundary of the lowy. When anyone left the lowy they left the special jurisdiction of Tonbridge (under the earl) and entered that of Kent (under the sheriff). Hugo's house could have been the 'Kent House' of Kent House Farm.

Keep ahead along Pierce Mill Lane. There is little traffic on this lane but watch out for cyclists coming fast round the bends!

Across the fields to the right and concealed by trees is Caxton Place, tentatively linked to the first English printer, William Caxton. He was born and brought up in the weald of Kent.

The farm became Simmons brewery in 1830 which operated until 1905. To provide clean water an artesian well about 860 ft deep was cut into the aquifer. Now it feeds storage reservoirs for irrigating the salad crops grown here in the summer.

When you arrive at the old mill workshop on your left, look out on your right for a footpath sign (Weald Way) concealed in the hedge. Go through a gate into a small yard and keep ahead following signs. Go through to a gravel drive and veer left to a grassy bank on the other side. Continue alongside a row of concrete mushrooms, now following the river Bourne upstream. Soon leave the garden and continue through scrubby woodland. Eventually pass a way-marked post and come out into the corner of a large arable field. Go along the left side of this field and look out on your left for a footbridge with metal rails. Cross over and continue directly ahead across the field to the hedge. Officially the path (Weald Way) goes through the hedge and back into this field (over two stiles and footbridges) but, if the

path is blocked or unclear, then keep the hedge on your right and follow it round. Whichever way you go, eventually you will follow a stream on your right and an old stone and brick wall. Arrive at a field gate with a gap and go through to Barnes Street.

There are some beautiful buildings in Barnes Street of mediaeval origin. Part of Barnes Place (opposite) is a two bay hall house possibly dating to the 13th century. Poplar Court on your right dates to the early 16th century.

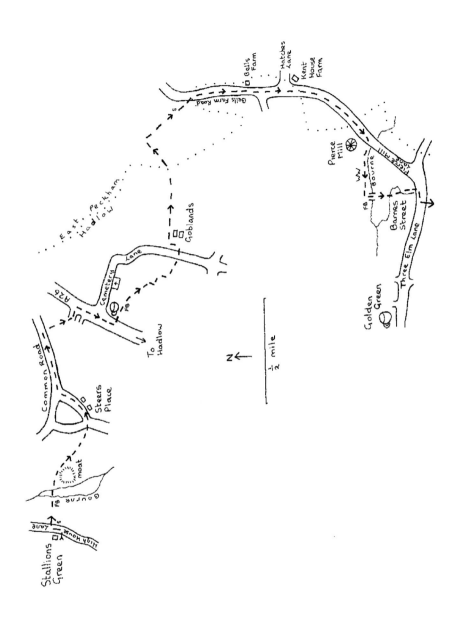

Stallions Green
High House Lane
FB
Bourne
moat
FB
Steers Place
Common Road
A26
To Hadlow
Cemetery Lane
FB
Goblands
East Peckham
Hadlow
Bells Farm Road
Bells Farm
Hatches Lane
Kent House Farm
Pierce Mill
Pierce Mill Road
Bourne
FB
Barnes Street
Three Elm Lane
Golden Green
N
½ mile

25

3

Barnes Street to Five Oak Green

Maps:	OS Explorer 136
Distance:	2 miles (mile 6)
Stiles:	2 stiles
Start:	Barnes Street; TQ 646482
Transport:	Bus 208 from Tonbridge
Refresh:	Pubs and shop, Five Oak Gr.
	The Bell. Golden Green

The Medway Valley is a low, flat country of lakes, streams, ditches and large unenclosed fields. There are huge skies and virtually no habitations. In the 13th century the nutritious meadows were used for fattening stock in drier seasons, the watercourses and river for fishing and ferrying.

'to the mill of John Curtone..so all the tenements of the Prior and of the Archbishop of Canterbury be without and so to Cnokewerespole and from there to wynelingbroke..'

The mill of John de Curtone may be Little Mill just to the east of Barnes Street. 'Cnokewerespole' translates as Oak Weir Pool and there is an Oak Weir Lock today where the parish boundary crosses the Medway. While not on this walk there is an opportunity to go there.

Cross the road to Barnes Place, turn right and then left along a track (Weald Way) to a stile. Go over the stile and continue ahead with a hay barn on your left. Turn left after the barn and go towards a farm entrance. Just before, turn right through a metal gate and join a footpath with beech trees on the right and a stream on the left. Continue, go through a gate and keep alongside the stream. Go through the next gate and continue with the stream still on your left. Cross another field in the same direction, go through a gate to Ford Green Bridge and cross over the river Medway.

Oak Weir Lock (cnokewerespole) is about half a mile downstream from here. Not well served with footpaths, it is not included on this walk but can be visited by going east (or left after the bridge) along the river and then returning to this point (30 minutes).

Tonbridge (4 miles) can be reached from here by turning right after the bridge and following the Weald Way (also see link walk 1).

Once across the bridge, turn left through a kissing gate then right to go in the direction of Five Oak Green. Go along the right side of the field and about 100 metres before the field end, bear right into a wood and continue to a stile. Go over, cross a footbridge and go forward to a lake. Keep the lake on your left

and follow an enclosed path to a hedge. Go through and cross a footbridge to a smaller lake. Turn left and follow the fence round to the other side of the lake until you reach a wooden railed footbridge on your left.

This remote area is completely free of houses and is left for fishing, agriculture and gravel works (now bird sanctuaries). It was a good place to set up a starfish bombing decoy in May 1942 where controlled fires deflected bombers from Tonbridge.

The footbridge crosses Hammer Dyke which is the boundary between Hadlow and Capel Parishes. Part of Capel was connected to the Manor of Hadlow and was therefore in the lowy of Tonbridge. The lowy boundary is about half a mile to the east (left). Ahead of you is a pronounced forested ridge. This upland area is the great 'South Frith' forest; another great hunting park of the Earl's to match that of the North Frith.

Cross over the footbridge and then in about 100 metres (just before the oak trees) the footpath splits in two. Fork left here so that the first oak tree is on your right. Keep ahead and soon the oasts of Moat Farm will come into view. Continue, and as you approach Moat Farm go left and then right across a footbridge. Turn left, keeping the farm buildings on your right.

Moat Farm had mediaeval origins and in among the modern industrial units there is an old farmhouse. It is on a slight hill and so for the first time since Barnes Street the land is dry enough to build on.

Go round the farm buildings keeping them on your right. Cross over a drive and go through a gap in the hedge. Turn right and keep the orchards on your left and hedge/windbreak on the right until you find yourself turning away from the farm buildings. At this point look out for a gap in the windbreak on your right, go through and across a footbridge to a drive. Turn left and continue along the drive to Whetsted Road. Turn right, go over the railway bridge and continue to the road junction at Five Oak Green. Cross over the road (Five Oak Green Road) to the shop.

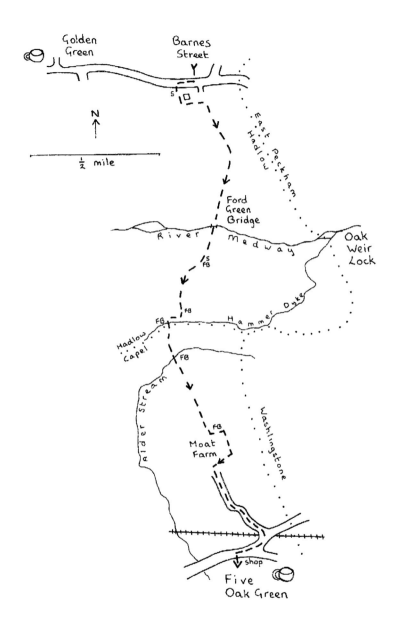

Golden Green

Barnes Street

N

½ mile

East Peckham Hadlow

Ford Green Bridge

River Medway

Oak Weir Lock

FB

Hammer Dyke

Hadlow Capel

FB

Alder Stream

FB

Washingstone

FB

Moat Farm

shop

Five Oak Green

© Crown copyright 2013 Ordnance Survey 100054134

29

4

Five Oak Green to Old Pembury

Maps:	OS Explorer 136
Distance:	2.5 miles (mile 8)
Stiles:	5 stiles
Start:	Village Shop; TQ 649454
Transport:	Bus 205 Tonbridge/F.O.Green
Parking:	Falmouth Place car park
Refresh:	Pubs and shop, Five Oak Green.
	The Dovecote, Alders Road

This walk follows the Alder Stream up towards the old forest of Tonbridge called the 'South Frith'. The hills of Pembury and Capel are covered with apple orchards and the woodland around Old Pembury is carpeted with bluebells and wild garlic in the spring.

'wynelingbroke is within..and so by the highway to Dodingebury which is without..the tenements of Wechelstone and Brenchesle are without..so west as far as the pale of the forest..'

The *'wynelingbroke'* is a 'winding' brook south of the Medway; the Alder Stream flowing through Five Oak Green is such a stream and has endowed many lands with the name of 'Brook.' This walk passes through the hundred of Washlingstone (from Alders Road) on its way west to the forest pale at Old Pembury, passing near 'Dodingebury' (Downingbury) on the way.

Facing the shop, turn right and in about 50 paces go left through an arch (between houses) joining an enclosed path. Continue past an orchard on the left and go up and down a small flight of steps over a bank. Continue along, cross a footbridge and a metal stile and pass a field on your right and the stream now on your left. At a path junction, hook left and eventually pass an oast house on your right. At the farm drive go straight across, turn left and then bear right between a house and farm buildings. Cross a footbridge where you join the stream again on its winding course. Cross another footbridge into a large hop field and go straight on for 100 metres.

Turn right over a stile by a barn, cross a footbridge and then another. Continue with a field on your right and a house on your left. At a drive, go straight across and continue, soon joining a high wooden fence on your left. Cross a stile and go directly ahead across the field eventually joining the right hedge. Follow it round to the right and come to the field corner. Turn left over a stile and go along an enclosed footpath, in front of the field hedge. Go through a gate, cross the next field by the right hedge and when it curves away to the right keep directly ahead. Emerge at Alders Road. There is a pub (The Dovecote Inn) on the right.

Cross the road and go over a stile opposite. Follow the right side of the field and at the end, turn left continuing round the edge of the same field, heading towards a wood. Keep straight ahead through the wood. When an orchard appears in front of you, bear right and go through a gate leading into it.

Follow signs, continuing uphill and aim for a gate in the far right corner. Go through, continue under electric cables and shortly turn right through a gate into Amhurst Bank Road. Turn left along the road passing Amhurst Hill Farm, and continue downhill to a bridge.

The Amhurst family were large landowners in the area in the 17th century. They lived at Bayhall near Pembury Green. Amhurst Hill Farm has old hop pickers' huts and cookhouses.

Immediately after the bridge turn right along a footpath through woods and look out left, for a way-marked post by a gate. Turn left through the gate and cross the field passing the buildings of Kent College on your right. Go into the next field through a gap. The path here is indistinct but head for the far right corner of the field where there is a gap into the next field.

The hill on the left topped with fir trees is Downingbury, the 'dodingebury' of the perambulation which was outside the lowy.

Keep alongside the fence on your right to the field end. Join a wooden walkway to a gate, go through and turn left to Old Church Road. Turn right for the church which though not open, is well worth a visit in any case.

In mediaeval times there were two Pembury Manors; Peppingbury Magna (Old Pembury) and Peppingbury Parva (Bayhall, just beyond Pembury Green). The lovely golden sandstone church is thought to have existed in the 12th century but additions were made by John Culpepper of Bayhall in the 14th century.

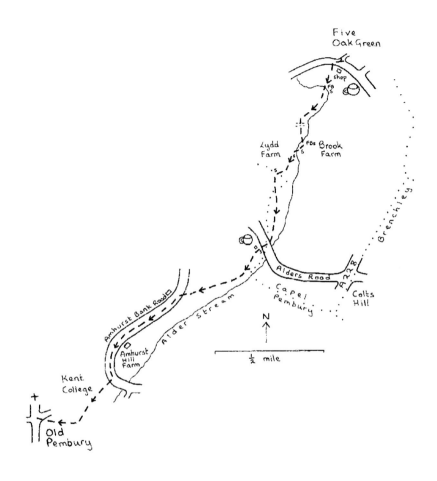

Five
Oak Green

shop
FB
s

Lydd
Farm

FBs   Brook
s   Farm

Grenchley

Alders Road

Capel
Pembury

Colts
Hill

Amhurst Bank Road

Alder Stream

N

½ mile

Amhurst
Hill
Farm

Kent
College

Old
Pembury

© Crown copyright 2013 Ordnance Survey 100054134

5

Old Pembury to Pembury Green

Maps:	OS Explorer 136
Distance:	2 miles (mile 10.5)
Stiles:	none
Start:	Pembury Old Church; TQ 626428
Transport:	Bus 208; Tonbridge/Pembury Green
Parking:	Pembury Old Church (limited)
Refresh:	Pubs and shops, Pembury High St.

An interesting and varied walk with pretty woodland paths, beginning in the still wooded 'South Frith' Forest of Tonbridge and finishing with some fine old buildings on Pembury High Street.

'and so as far as the pale of the forest ..and so by the pale so the land which is the fee of the earl is within..'

The forest pale of the 'South Frith' (the old Tonbridge Parish boundary) is conveniently followed by a public footpath just inside its curved course. You will pass the site of an old forest gate, now a major road junction.

Start

Start at St Peter's Church, Old Pembury, and walk down Old Church Road passing Kent College and Pembury Waterworks on your left. Continue up towards the A228 Maidstone Road joining the pavement on the left after Redwings Lane. At the junction with the Maidstone Road follow the pavement round to the left and spiral uphill crossing the footbridge over the road. Go forward for a few paces and then turn right on a footpath which runs alongside the road. Arrive at a gate and turn left in front of it along a path enclosed with high wire fences. This is the line of the old forest pale.

The footpath hardly changes direction as it follows the course of the forest fence. Near the beginning it takes a dog leg turn where it switches from one side of the boundary bank to the other. This bank can be seen, mainly on your left. This wood is called 'Forest Wood' meaning the wood of Tonbridge Forest.

Continue along, passing pine plantations, coppiced chestnut and silver birch. Eventually pass school grounds and a small graveyard on your left. Continue along and when houses come near to the path, bear right across a wide wooden footbridge. Ignore the next path on the right and come to a major path junction. Keep straight on and go uphill passing houses on the left and woods on the right. Pass an incoming path from the right. Continue ahead and go round a large gate and eventually emerge on the busy junction of the Maidstone Road and the old Tonbridge/Hastings Road.

This junction is called Woodsgate, once a gated entrance to the 'South Frith.' The gate went across a much narrower version of Pembury High Street. From Woodsgate, the old forest boundary continued in the direction of Tunbridge Wells although the precise course is uncertain.

Here you leave the forest pale and go towards Pembury Green which was part of the hundred of Washlingstone and was outside the lowy. The Clares tried on more than one occasion to include it in the lowy of Tonbridge.

Turn next left past the petrol station and continue along Pembury High Street to Pembury Green and the Camden Arms.

Pembury High Street was the old Hastings to London Road before the A21 By-Pass was constructed and was once busy with stagecoaches and other traffic. As a result there are some handsome houses lining the way with their 'mews' (stables). Occasional 'cul de sacs' with new houses have replaced former mews or gardens.

Across the road from the 'Camden Arms' there is a horse trough on the green which commemorates the martyrdom of Marjorie Polley in 1555. She was burnt at the stake in Tonbridge for her Protestant faith.

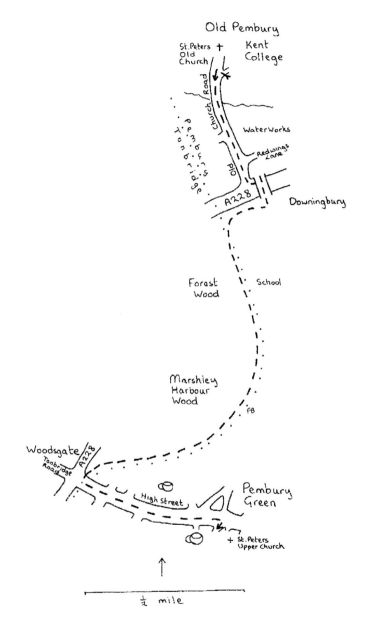

37

6

Pembury Green to Tunbridge Wells

Maps:	OS Explorer 136
Distance:	3.5 miles (mile 12.5)
Stiles:	2 stiles (can be avoided)
Start:	Pembury Green; TQ 625407
Transport:	Bus 208; Tonbridge/Pembury Gr.
	Bus 6/6A; T Wells/Pembury Gr.
Parking:	Pembury Green
Refresh:	Pubs,Cafes and Shops, Tunbridge Wells

This is a walk of contrasts, starting in the country with glorious views and ending in Tunbridge Wells High Street with its buzzing cafes, pubs and shops. The

approximate course of the South Frith forest pale can be seen most of the way and in Tunbridge Wells, the most southerly point of the perambulation is reached.

'and so by the pale to Bromelegeregg which is all within..and Sunningelegh and Hocubery of the service of the King be without..and so to the oak called Wogebohe..'

'Bromelegeregg,' meaning 'broom ridge' suggests an open heathland from which we now have High Brooms. It probably referred to the ridge on which the A264 Pembury Road runs. This road continues to Crescent Road in Tunbridge Wells where there was a small Tudor hamlet called Bromelerge.

38

Sunningelegh (Sunninglye) is the name of a farm near Frant and Hocubery is modern Hawkenbury through which this walk passes.

The oak tree of 'wogeboh' could have been at the meeting point of parish and county boundaries at the church of King Charles the Martyr. Prominent or distinctive trees were often used as boundary markers.

Start at Pembury Green, pass the Camden Arms on your right and then turn right down Chalket Lane. St Peter's Upper Church is on your left.

The church was consecrated in 1847 and in 1886 a 92 foot spire was added, lasting 100 years. Demolished when crumbling stonework aroused safety concerns; it must have been a significant landmark.

Continue down Chalket Lane, go through a pair of open white gates and come to a white gate on your left (to avoid the two stiles and livestock on this walk continue down Chalket Lane to a path junction at the bottom of the hill and then pick up the directions at ** next page). Turn left in front of the gate of Great Bayhall House and continue on an enclosed path.

Keep ahead in roughly the same direction and eventually you will come alongside the A21 immediately on your right, in a deep cutting. Continue to the footbridge on your right and cross over the A21. Go straight on following a high wooden fence on your left and wood on your right. Follow the fence round to the right, ignoring a path going left and continue ahead to a path junction with good views from the field gate.

The ridge over to the right is the approximate course of the South Frith forest pale and 'Bromelegeregg.' The farm on the hill in front of you is Little Bayhall Farm which you will pass on this walk.

Turn right at the junction in the direction of the Tunbridge Wells Circular Walk (TWCW). Continue along a wide track and after about 100 metres turn left over a stile into a field. Go downhill straight across the field taking a course in the direction of the high farm on the opposite hill, then aim for a tall clump of trees and continue to the bottom of the field. At the field edge, cross a stile and a footbridge then turn right along a track (Chalket Lane). Take the next left along a track through woods, following the TWCW.

** (If you came all the way down Chalket Lane, turn right through woodland along a track following the 'Tunbridge Wells Circular Walk').

Continue ahead and go uphill on the right side of a field. Continue through a gateway onto a paved lane (High Woods Lane). Pass cottages on your right and continue along the lane through Little Bayhall Farm.

The river in the valley on your left is the Teise which is the Kent/Sussex county boundary. There was once a grand country house called Bayhall with formal gardens in the valley. You can see a painting of it hanging up in Tunbridge Wells Museum. The site, which was once a mediaeval moat, was the home of the Culpeppers who may have taken their name from an old form of Pembury (Peppingeberia, 12th century). Eventually they moved away and were followed by the Amhurst and the Camden families whose names can be found in buildings, roads and pubs nearby.

Continue along the lane until you eventually pass the Royals Indoor Bowls Club on your right. Go round the gated entrance and continue along High Woods Lane passing 'Marl Pits allotments' on your right.

Marl Pits are a common feature in the landscape. By the 13th century and before artificial fertilisers, marl was often dug out of pits to spread on fields. Believed to be lime rich, it was used in areas far from chalk.

Continue to a T junction, turn left and soon reach the busy Forest Road. Keep left and continue round Forest Road, passing a shop and a church on your left at Hawkenbury. Continue to the island crossing, cross over Forest Road, turn right and then left along a 'no through road' (Camden Park).

This is Hawkenbury (Hocubury), the land on the perambulation belonging to the King and just outside the lowy of Tonbridge.

Continue ahead as the road becomes a footpath, passing fields on your right. Emerge onto a road, turn right and after a few paces turn left along a

Restricted Byway just after houses called Hollyshaw Close. Come out at Claremont School and go past the entrance, then keep ahead along a path to the right of Glen Cottage. Arrive at a T junction with Claremont Road, cross over and turn left.

Claremont Road is not an old name but it is very appropriate on this hill belonging once to the Clares of Tonbridge Castle.

Pass Norfolk, Grecian and Buckingham Roads on your right and then turn right into Grove Park. Continue down the left side of the park.

Grove Park was a gift from the Villiers family in 1703 to the Wells. They lived at Somerhill and were owners of the South Frith (which had become a manor and extended from Tonbridge to Tunbridge Wells).

Keep ahead and leave the park down a narrow cobbled street called South Grove. Emerge onto the High Street and turn left continuing along a raised pavement. At the end, go straight on along a pedestrian street towards the church of King Charles the Martyr. Turn right in front of the church and continue round to the entrance.

Open to the public, 11am to 3pm each day, this delightful church is worth a visit for the handsome baroque ceilings among many other things. Go past the church entrance to the south wall, where in the brick work below the second window you can see the Tonbridge and Speldhurst Parish boundary (also marked on the opposite and inside walls).

Away from the church wall, a boundary stone is set in the pavement, marking the county and parish boundaries. Perhaps the oak tree of 'Wogebohe' was here at the southern end of the lowy. In the 13th century it was still very rural with a stream (now buried under paving), bubbling springs and large trees intermingled with rocky outcrops.

Across the road from here and just within the Pantiles is the Chalybeate (iron rich) spring which Lord North discovered had healing powers in 1606 and so began the extraordinary growth of Tunbridge Wells.

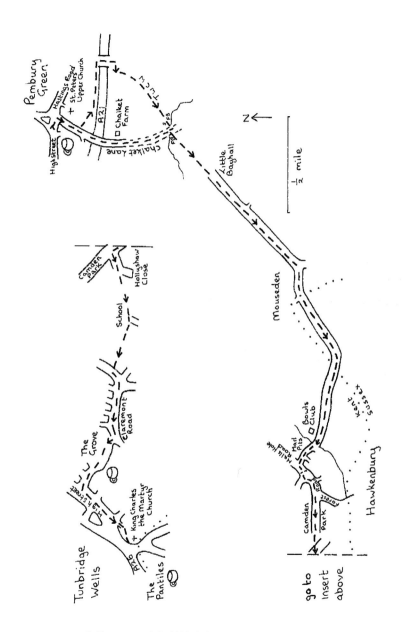

7

Tunbridge Wells to Stockland Green

Maps:	OS Explorer 147
Distance:	3 miles (mile 16)
Stiles:	3 stiles
Start:	Neville Street; TQ 582388
Transport:	Trains & Buses; Tonbridge/T.Wells
Parking:	Tunbridge Wells
Refresh:	Tunbridge Wells; Pubs, Cafes and Shops.

Walk the red brick pavements of Tunbridge Wells then change to woodland paths in dappled shade, fast flowing streams and high green pastures.

'and so to the domus of Willelmi de Colverdene within..and through the middle of the wood of Hertesell so all the tenants of Wechelstone are without..'

The perambulation is followed almost exactly. Hugging the old Tonbridge/Speldhurst Parish boundary it leaves the South Frith and skirts round the 'South Borough.' The land of William of Colverden, still exists in the numerous 'Culverden' street names.

Start

Start at the boundary stone set in paving outside the church of King Charles the Martyr and cross Neville Street. Turn right and cross London Road to 'The Forum,' *(built as public 'rest rooms' in 1939 and now a popular music venue).* Walk up the right side of 'The Forum' and at a T junction turn right and continue straight on, until you emerge again on London Road. Cross at the island, turn left and bear right along the red brick pavement of the Inner London Road.

The Inner London Road is the old Tonbridge Parish and lowy boundary. To the right was the great South Frith forest and the area of Bromelegeregg on the perambulation (see notes on p38). South Frith became a manor and part of the Somerhill Estate. Somerhill and its owners are seen in house and road names along the Inner London Road.

Tunbridge Wells is built on sandstone and between here and Speldhurst are massive walls made of it and solitary outcrops.

Continue directly ahead passing Church Road, York Road, Dudley Road and Lime Hill Road. Cross Mount Ephraim Road and continue along Mount Ephraim and then cross over via the pelican crossing. Turn left and go back along Mount Ephraim and then right down Royal Chase.

The perambulation continues along Royal Chase away from the South Frith and now skirts round the 'South Borough' of Tonbridge. To the right is Culverden, belonging in the 13th century to William of Colverden.

Go straight on at the crossroads, down Byng Road. At the T junction, turn right along Culverden Down, going down and then up. Just before Coniston Avenue, switchback left along a footpath down to a stream. Follow the stream on your left and emerge at the other end of Coniston Avenue.

Go forward to an unmade road alongside a high wire fence. With the fence on your left, pass a waterworks building and then fork right along the wider track through Hurst Wood.

The name Hurst Wood may come from Speldhurst. The wood is within the parish and the perambulation route is picked up again on leaving it at Broomhill Road. The steep gradients in the wood are typical of the sandstone geology in this southern half of the lowy of Tonbridge.

Continue to a kissing gate, go through and fork right uphill along the widest track. Keep straight on and look out for an old iron gatepost buried in a beech tree on your right. Eventually cross a stile by a metal gate and continue along an enclosed path. At a path junction bear left downhill, go over a stream and continue up a narrow path to Broomhill Road. Turn right and Salomons Tower will come into view as well as the next hill to climb.

Salomons is now a campus of Christ Church University, Canterbury but in 1855 it was the home of David Salomons, Lord Mayor of London and one of the founders of the predecessor of the Nat West Bank. His nephew David Lionel was a scientist and he carried out many electrical experiments at the estate after he inherited it in 1873. He installed one of the first domestic electric lighting systems, powered by a coal fired generator.

You will follow the perambulation for the rest of the walk with Tonbridge on your right and Speldhurst in Washlingstone hundred on your left.

Continue down Broomhill Road, pass the entrance to Mill Farm and turn left just in front of a high stone wall. Continue alongside a stream on this enclosed path, eventually leaving it and ascending the hill with glimpses of Speldhurst over on the left.

The name Speldhurst is first recorded in the 8th century as belonging to the Bishop of Rochester. The village was an important centre of Washlingstone hundred and perhaps for this reason remained outside the lowy, despite the nearness of the land hungry and powerful Norman Clares.

At the top of the hill arrive at a road (Speldhurst Road), cross over and go up stone steps and through a kissing gate to join a narrow enclosed footpath. Continue to a kissing gate, go through to a T junction and turn left on the Tunbridge Wells Circular Walk (TWCW). At the next kissing gate, go through into a field and turn right leaving the TWCW and joining the Wealdway (WW). Go along the right side of the field to the corner. Cross over a stile and then continue across the next field. Go over another stile and follow an enclosed path to emerge on Stockland Green Road. Turn left to the junction with Franks Hollow Road.

To go to Speldhurst (about a mile including a steep hill) continue down Stockland Green Road, turn right at 'The Forge' and continue along the WW to Speldhurst (consult OS map). To rejoin the perambulation you would need to retrace your steps to Franks Hollow Road.

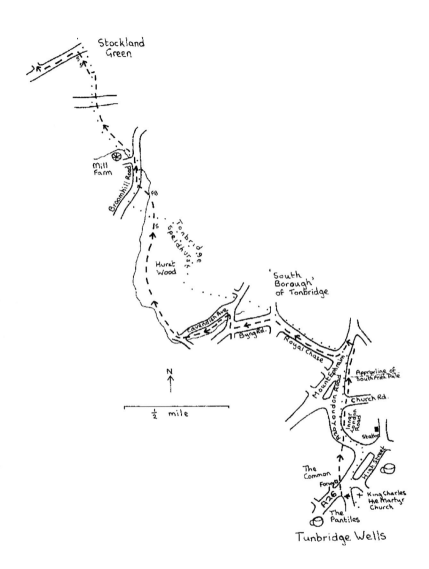

48

8

Stockland Green to Penshurst

Maps:	OS Explorer 147
Distance:	3 miles (mile 19)
Stiles:	12 stiles
Start:	Franks Hollow Road; TQ 564420
Parking:	Stockland Green (limited)
Refresh:	Cafes and shops, Penshurst

A gentle walk, mostly downhill with a picture postcard panorama throughout; first Bidborough Ridge, then Speldhurst Hill and the Medway Valley with Smarts Hill beyond. In between there are some fascinating old houses and farms and at the end, Penshurst Place and village.

'and so through the middle of the wood of Hertesell so all the tenants of Wechelstone are without..and directly to the messuage of William Shrufin..and so to Wolstonesland and Horgate and Hegedonne..to a sort of hill called Smethedonne..'

Topographic details such as the middle of a wood or a hill help in identifying places. You will follow the perambulation route along Bentham Brook Valley, passing Shrufin's place, Stone Wood and 'Hegedonne.'

Start at Stockland Green and go down Franks Hollow Road with good views across to Bidborough Ridge. Pass the entrance to Scriventon House on your left and continue downhill to where the road turns sharply right. Here, turn left over a stile and cross a field with views across Bentham Brook to Bidborough Ridge. At the far left corner of the field, go over a stile and continue along the left side of the next field. At the corner, cross a stile, bear right across the yard and go over a brick and stone stile.

You are passing through Scriventon Farm, named after Shrufin (sc is pronounced sh in Old English); 'ton' is a later addition meaning place or farm. The boundary of the lowy followed the brook, so William's house was 'without,' on the Speldhurst side.

Pass a barn on your right and continue downhill along a paved track, looking ahead to the Medway Valley with Speldhurst Hill on your left. As you approach the valley bottom cross a footbridge and bear right. Follow a stream on your right and look out for another stream joining (Bentham Brook) along which is the Tonbridge boundary.

From this confluence, the old Tonbridge boundary joins you on the track for a short stretch before going left just before the wood. Passing the wood on your left, you are now in the lowy of Tonbridge and the jurors probably walked this same path from Scriventon. Woodland on the right is called Little Tonbridge Wood.

Continue along the track to a row of houses. Cross the stile and continue between houses to Barden Road. Turn left and then next right along a drive towards Barden Furnace Farm and Old Barn. Continue ahead, leaving the drive as it bears right, on an enclosed track to a stile. Cross and go straight on along the left side of the field, passing ponds on your left. Over to the right you can see the buildings of Barden Furnace Farm and Mill.

This once part of Tonbridge (now in Bidborough) is centred on Barden Mill. It was connected with Barden Park and both areas are thought to have once belonged to Eynsford Manor but became part of the lowy of Tonbridge with the arrival of the Normans.

There was a mill here in 1086 and an ironworks could have been here in mediaeval times. Iron, timber and plentiful, fast flowing water were available to encourage a local iron industry. It supplied arms for the Parliamentary Army in the English Civil War.

Along the route there are a number of ponds on the left side of the path. It is possible that they were all connected to the mill as holding ponds for water. At times when the water level in the stream was low the ponds could be emptied in sequence to allow the mill wheel to continue turning.

Stone Wood on the left could be a shortened form of 'Wolstonesland.'

51

Continue along the left side of fields and eventually cross a stile to a pond. Continue on the right side of the pond and go over another stile. Keep ahead passing between two telegraph poles and join a field hedge on your left. Continue to the next corner and go over a stile. Pass another pond on your left and continue along the left side of the field to the next corner.

Over to the right there is a very distinct conical hill, which on tithe maps is called High Dens. It is the Hegedenne of the perambulation and is within the lowy.

Go over a stile and down steps to the road (Penshurst Road) at Poundsbridge. Turn right to the junction.

The house at Poundsbridge has a date of 1593 and the initials WD (William Durkinghole). Durkinghole is a family name long associated with the local area and in the perambulation it is mentioned twice associated with property in the area of Penshurst and Chiddingstone Causeway.

Continue along the road (now Poundsbridge Lane) passing a red pillar box on your right, cross a bridge over Bentham Brook and then pass Bowens Cottage on your left and Bowens Farm on your right.

Bowens Farm could be the approximate site of 'horgate' (without) since the old Tonbridge boundary passes uphill of the farm, across the lane and on obliquely up the hill. At the top of the hill on the road, is an old smithy and perhaps there was one here in 1279. The hill was a source of timber and iron ore and if there was mediaeval iron working at Barden, it is also likely that a smith would set up shop on the road and give the hill its name 'smethedonne.'

Turn left just before the next house on your left and enter a small drive. Go through a field gate and continue along the right side of the field to the corner. Go over a stile and continue ahead and then left along an enclosed path to a junction in front of a pair of gates. Turn right and continue to Old Swaylands manor house. Pass the house on your left, then turn left along a track passing the ivy clad 'Stone Cottage' on your right. Go directly ahead along the enclosed path following a high brick wall. At a gate, go through and continue alongside the grounds of Swaylands on your right.

The Tonbridge boundary passed through Swaylands and on up the hill. The fields going down to the Medway on your left were once hop gardens and you can still see occasional hop poles in the hedges.

At a metal gate, go through and continue ahead along the track, eventually bearing right and following a fence on your left.

Penshurst is now visible across the Medway. The river turns a corner here and the valley has narrowed enough to make a good crossing place.

Continue to a metal gate, go through and emerge on a road (Rogues Hill). Turn left, cross over two bridges and arrive at the entrance to Penshurst Place. Tonbridge can be reached by turning right here (5 miles along the Eden Valley Walk, see link walk 2) or continue on the perambulation.

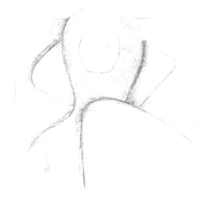

Penshurst was a grand house and garden even in 1279. It was the seat of Sir Stephen of Pencestre, one of three judges presiding over the perambulation. There is a very fine 14th century hall, but nothing remains of Stephen's home, only his garden, and his effigy in Penshurst Church.

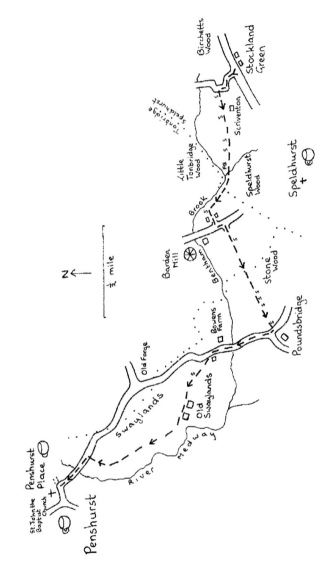

54

Penshurst to Chiddingstone Causeway

Maps:	OS Explorer 147
Distance:	2 miles (mile 22)
Stiles:	3 stiles
Start:	Entrance Penshurst Place; TQ 528438
Transport:	Trains; Tonbridge/Penshurst.
	Penshurst Station is in Chid.Causeway.
Parking:	Penshurst Place and Village
Refresh:	Cafes and shops, Penshurst; Little Brown Jug, C.C.

Gentle gradients, green fields, parkland and exotic woods accompany you on this walk making up for nearly half a mile of quite a busy road. Visit Penshurst Place, its beautiful gardens and the church if time allows.

'to the garden of Penecestr and directly to Redelef..and from Redelef to Durkynghale..'

Penshurst and Redleaf still exist today, but Durkynghale is hard to trace. In old deeds the name is associated with the Eden Valley at Chiddingstone, where parish boundaries met and was likely to be disputed territory. The perambulation follows the Leigh Parish boundary.

Start outside the entrance arch to Penshurst Place facing the village. Turn right up steps to pass through the picturesque buildings of 'Leicester Square' and continue to the entrance of the Church.

Leicester Square is a pleasing mix of old 16th century and newer 1850 buildings (by George Devey, architect). The Church is open during the day and inside the Sidney Chapel there is an effigy of Sir Stephen of Penshurst lying on the floor. He is in chain mail with his hand on the hilt of his sword

as if to draw. As Constable of Dover Castle and Lord Warden of the Cinque Ports and a justice in the King's service, he presided over the perambulation in Tonbridge. He must have had a grand house in Penshurst although none of it remains.

Continue past the church on your right and go through a kissing gate into Penshurst Park. Follow the wooden fence on your right and where the path forks, keep ahead. Again where there is another fork, keep ahead passing left of a group of conifers. Come to a kissing gate, cross the drive and go through another kissing gate opposite. Continue ahead through an avenue of trees passing a cricket ground on your right. At the end of the cricket ground follow the track as it bears right between two trees. Continue going slightly left so that you will go alongside the avenue of trees on your left. Pass large oaks on your right and continue to a kissing gate ahead. Go through and continue straight uphill aiming at a house on the hilltop and woodland higher up on the left.

Over to the far right is the ancient Sidney Oak thought to be nearly 500 years old and planted at the birth of Sir Philip Sidney. The Sidney family, now Viscounts de Lisle (once Earls of Leicester) have owned Penshurst since 1552. It was recently named as one of the 50 greatest British trees.

Continue uphill alongside the wood towards the top left corner of the park. As you approach the corner, look out for and go over a stile in the left fence. Continue through trees and go over another stile to emerge at Redleaf Cottage. Turn left to Penshurst Road, turn right and continue along the road with care. Pass Wells View, Redleaf House and North Lodge.

The perambulation and parish boundary goes 'directly' to Redleaf (Redelef), crossing the road from Penshurst Park and continuing between Redleaf House and North Lodge.

Redleaf today is noted for the exotic trees planted in the grounds and neighbouring woods. William Wells (shipbuilder) who resided there in the

early 19th century was the most important patron of the artist, Edwin Landseer (who painted animals including the famous stag, 'Monarch of the Glen'). He had a large collection of Landseer's paintings, now dispersed. His successor (also William Wells) was a champion rifle shot and set up a volunteer rifle range in Penshurst Park which is marked on old O.S. Maps.

Continue along Penshurst Road, passing a road junction, then in about 200 metres turn left through a gate into Redleaf Wood. Continue and go straight ahead at a junction with a forest track. Go more or less directly ahead (as much as the winding path allows) and you will descend gradually towards a  footbridge at the bottom of the wood. Go over a stile and then the footbridge to emerge at the corner of a field.

You are now in Durkynghale country. There is a 13th century deed in which Stephen of Penshurst allows William de Durkynghale to overwinter his sheep on common land here. Durkynghale is a name found commonly in the area from the 13th century onwards, eventually becoming shortened to Durtnall. In old deeds the name is associated with the river Eden, nearly a mile downstream of here.

Turn left and go alongside the stream on your left until you reach Moorden Farm buildings. Go past an open barn on your left and then turn left in front of a beech hedge to follow the track to the road. At the road (Station Hill) turn right and then fork left just after Moorden Oast. Continue to the car park at Penshurst Station.

You are walking through an extended part of Leigh Parish as the boundary swings west (left) to the river Eden. Durkynghale lands were in this area and were disputed lands as they seemed to straddle the Leigh/Penshurst/Chiddingstone boundaries and were intermingled with lands of the Archbishop and the Clares.

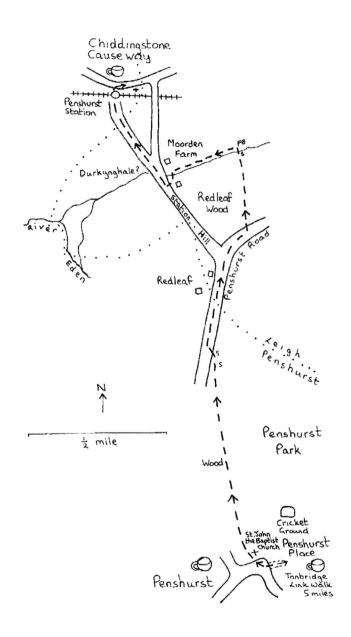

© Crown copyright 2013 Ordnance Survey 100054134

Chiddingstone Causeway to Nizels

Maps:	OS Explorer 147
Distance:	3 miles (mile 24)
Stiles:	7 stiles
Start:	Penshurst Station; TQ 519465
Transport:	Trains; Tonbridge/Penshurst
	Penshurst Station is in Chid. Causeway
Parking:	Chid. Causeway or on the Penshurst side of
	the station where there is a car park.
Refresh:	Little Brown Jug, Chid. Causeway;
	The Greyhound, Charcott; Pubs in Weald

This is wealden clay country, gently ascending northwards towards the greensand ridge. The heavy clays seem intractable when ploughed but it is fertile land where cereals are grown in large rolling fields. In among them streams weave through copses and there are glorious views throughout.

'through the middle of Rissettes to Coppingsland and so next to the land of the Prior of Tonbridge which is within..and so to the mead of Newsoles..'

From the start the Leigh Parish boundary curves north eastwards, nearly to Weald, and footpaths follow it all the way round a large area called Coppings, then Priory Farm and a little further on, Nizels. These place names next door to each other, have survived for over seven centuries.

Start

From the car park at Penshurst Station (on the other side of the railway from the Little Brown Jug), go over the footbridge and exit the station. Cross over the road to the Little Brown Jug, turn right and go uphill passing St. Luke's Church over on the right. Turn left along a tarmac footpath opposite a road junction and continue to the next road (Camp Hill).

The huge fields on the right were once the site of Penshurst Airfield during the two World Wars. In peacetime it was used for light aircraft and as an emergency landing strip for civil aircraft. The Leigh Parish boundary runs along this path, making this the most likely perambulation route. In the 13th century this area was called 'Herrings Heath' and the fields were still called Herringslands on c1840 tithe maps.

At Camp Hill, turn right and first left towards Charcott. Keep straight ahead, leaving the road along a track signed Charcott Farm. Pass Little Keepers on your right and shortly turn right through a gate. Bear left across the field passing buildings on your left. Continue to a kissing gate, go through and keep ahead, alongside a hedge on your left. At the hedge corner descend on a grassy track to Wickhurst Brook.

The long curving hedge on your left which stays with you for much of this walk is the Leigh Parish boundary.

Cross the footbridge, go uphill and continue until you rejoin the boundary hedge, keeping it on your left. Go through a gap in the field corner and continue straight alongside the hedge. At the point where the hedge ends, go straight on towards a wood.

61

Keep on the left side of the wood and eventually cross a footbridge. Turn right then immediately left uphill, following the fence on your left. Continue through another field, now following a line of trees on your left. Arrive at a clump of trees concealing a pond. Skirt round the right side of the pond to a corner. Turn right and follow the hedge on your left, looking out for a metal gate in the hedge line.

The field on your right is called 'Coppingsfield' on tithe maps and is part of a large estate centred on Coppings Farm. The Leigh Parish boundary

continues along the hedge on your left going towards Priory Farm, once belonging to Tonbridge Priory. The priory is now buried under the railway station and car parks.

Turn left through the gate, go straight across the field to a corner and then follow an enclosed grassy path with a lake on your right. Bear left, joining a stony track and then leave the track, continuing along a narrow enclosed path. Continue through woods and an adventure playground. Eventually go down steps to Hale Oak Road and turn right past Brook Cottage.

Continue for about a quarter mile and look for a metal stile on your right, entering a field. Go through, cross the field and go over a footbridge. Climb steps up to a gate, go through and cross the next field uphill, passing a telegraph pole and oak tree. Head for a way-marked gate, go through and cross the farm track to another gate. Go through and continue along the left side of the field to a kissing gate. Continue on the left side of the next field to another kissing gate. Go through passing a garden on your right to Scabharbour Road at Fletchers Green.

Turn left and then right down Egg Pie Lane. In about 50 metres turn left over a stile and follow the right side of a long field passing a pond behind a post and rail fence on your right. Aim for the far left corner and go over a stile. Follow a hedge on your right and continue to a way-marked gate and stile in the hedge line.

You are now at the boundary of the lowy and Tonbridge Parish, in a large area called Nizels, a place recorded in the perambulation as 'Newsoles.'

There is a choice now: either go on the shortest route to the next stage (11) or go to Weald via a boundary stone.

Shortest route: Turn right through the gate/stile, follow the Tonbridge boundary hedge on your left and turn left with the hedge, continuing to a footbridge on the left. Cross over and go forward to a stile on your right. Go over and continue through a tunnel beneath the railway to Nizels Golf Course. Continue with the next stage on page 65.

To the boundary stone and Weald: Pass the stile on your right and keep straight ahead going through a gateway with the Tonbridge boundary hedge on your right. Keep ahead to a stile. Go over and cross the next field to another stile where, behind the fence and to the right, is the boundary stone.

This stone marks the meeting of Tonbridge, Leigh and Weald (once Sevenoaks) Parishes. Such a significant place in the perambulation was probably recorded. Flat and criss-crossed with streams it fits the description of 'Newsoles' (Nizels) mead, within the lowy.

To continue to Weald, go over the stile and follow the hedge on your right to the next corner. Go over a stile and keep ahead along a gated track to Morleys Road and a pub (Edwards). Turn left for the village.

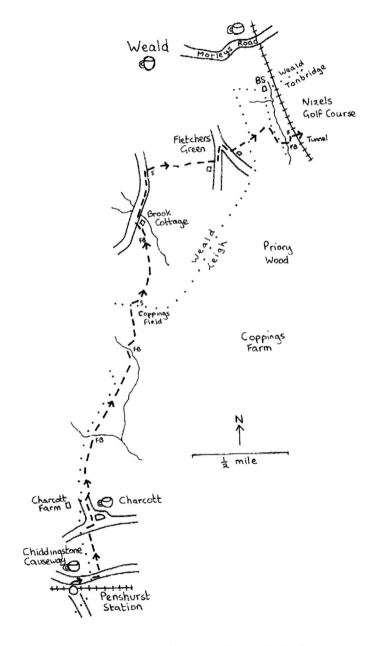

Weald

Morleys Road

BS

Weald
Tonbridge

Nizels
Golf Course

Fletchers
Green

S

Tunnel

FB

Brook
Cottage

FB

Weald
Leigh

Priory
Wood

S

Coppings
Field

FB

Coppings
Farm

N

½ mile

FB

FB

Charcott
Farm

Charcott

Chiddingstone
Causeway

Penshurst
Station

Nizels to Underriver

Maps:	OS Explorer 147
Distance:	3 miles (mile 27)
Stiles:	7 stiles
Start:	Nizels Golf Course; TQ 539503
Transport:	Bus 402 to Weald
Parking:	Weald (half mile to start)
Refresh:	Pubs in Weald
	The White Rock, Underriver

From here to the end of the walk at Shipbourne, the greensand ridge on the northern edge of the weald is a dramatic backdrop to gentle pastures and bluebell woods. The perambulation and the lowy of Tonbridge are entirely in the weald.

'and so to the mead of Newsoles which is within..and so to the paved way and to Romdshedde..so the fee of the Earl is within..'

Newsoles is Nizels, famous now for its golf and leisure club. The 'paved way' has to be the London Road which is an ancient route through Tonbridge and is followed for a while. Romshed Farm still exists and is an old moat site through which the Tonbridge boundary passes.

To start from Weald; With 'The Windmill' on your right continue along the road and then Morleys Road (passing through crossroads) to a pub (Edwards) on your left. Just after the pub and Elses Farm on your right, turn right through a kissing gate and along a track. Keep ahead and go over a stile into a field. Continue along the left side of the field to a stile and a boundary stone (*see notes on page 63*). Go over the stile and bear left towards the railway and field corner. Cross a footbridge and then veer left over another footbridge into the next field. Walk alongside the railway until you come to a tunnel going under on the left. Go over the stile and through the tunnel to Nizel's Golf Course.

Start

Emerge from the railway tunnel and go forward to a stony track and continue ahead, passing Hole 3 on your left. Keep straight on, leaving the track, and soon turn right over a footbridge at a way-marked post. Go uphill alongside a wood on your left and at the end, go directly across the golf course to a pond. Keep the pond on your left and go through a gate to Nizels Lane. Turn left along the lane passing Nizels Farm on your right and the entrance to the Golf Club on your left. Go across the road bridge over the A21 to London Road.

The original Nizels manor house was destroyed by fire in 1899. It was rebuilt, sold and opened as a Golf and Leisure Club in 1992. The A21 Sevenoaks to Tonbridge By-Pass was opened by The Right Hon Edward Heath PM, in 1971. Local residents remember the problems caused by the wealden clay which walkers know plenty about. London Road (the paved way) was the first turnpike road in Kent to be opened in 1709.

Cross over London Road and turn left. Pass Bank Lane on your right and the motel on your left and continue to Morley's roundabout.

Morleys is named after a farm of that name just by the road. The motel started life as Morley's farm hut where teas and farm produce were sold.

Pass St Julian's cottage on the right and turn right along a restricted by-way just before St Julian's Lodge. Go through woodland for about half a mile.

To the left is Riverhill which is a tautological name because the river comes from 'rither' (Old English for hill), so the name means 'hill hill'. St. Julian's lodge is the beginning of a large estate which used to be called Romdshedde Manor as in the perambulation. Much of the estate is now called St. Julian's after a house built in the 19th century, but Romshed Farm through which you will pass, still preserves the old name. There is a story that a William Rumsched found a poor boy in Sevenoaks in the 14th century and adopted him, calling him William Sevenoke. He was later to become Lord Mayor of London and founder of Sevenoaks School.

Turn right through a kissing gate into Romshed Farm lands. Go along the left side of the field to the corner. Turn left to a gate with a stile.

This stile is on the Tonbridge and Sevenoaks boundary and was probably crossed by the jurors on the perambulation. They would have continued ahead as the boundary did, through the farm buildings and perhaps paused a while for refreshment, who knows?

Go over the stile and cross the field towards the right side of the farm buildings and at the corner go over a stile, cross the farm drive and over another stile. Turn left across the field towards a pond and a field gate.

The pond is near a moat site on which there was probably a house in the 13th century. The perambulation route came straight through the middle of Romshed manor (spelt in many different ways and even now has an alternative spelling of Rumshott) as the parish and constituency boundary does today.

At the gate, cross the stile and go directly ahead to another gate and go over the stile (*the Tonbridge boundary turns right along the hedge here*). Go straight uphill across the field passing left of a telegraph pole. At a gate, go through and follow an enclosed path, then turn right following the fence round and go through light wood to a recreation ground. Keep along the right side to the corner and go over a stile to the road (Carters Hill) at Underriver. Turn right to continue the walk or left for the White Rock Inn.

Underriver means 'under the hill' and certainly the greensand ridge dominates the village so that it looks almost 'alpine'. The beauty of the area drew artists such as Samuel Palmer (1805-1881) who painted and sketched a number of landscapes from the top of the hill or lower down in the vicinity of the village. Local

residents have written a book on his work entitled, 'Underriver; Samuel Palmer's Golden Valley' by Griselda Barton with Michael Tong.

68

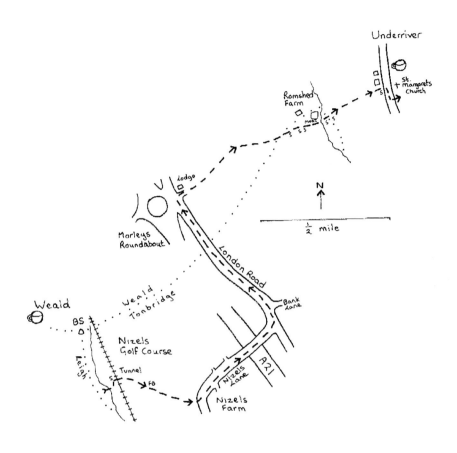

Underriver to Shipbourne

Maps:	OS Explorer 147
Distance:	3 miles (mile 30)
Stiles:	12 stiles
Start:	St. Margarets Church, Underriver; TQ 556520
Parking:	Underriver
Refresh:	The White Rock, Underriver
	The Chaser Inn, Shipbourne

Beginning in pleasant pastures with the greensand hills still to the north, the last part of the walk finishes on a long straight section along the course of the forest pale of the 'North Frith,' where farms give way to bluebell woods.

'so the fee of the Earl is within and Holindenne without..and so directly to the pale of the forest so the tenements of the Earl are always within..and so by the pale of the forest to Somegate..'

South of Underriver there is a large area of land called Hollanden which was outside the lowy of Tonbridge. The perambulation diverted south from Underriver, visiting places in Hollanden to confirm the boundaries.

Individual locations are elusive but Hollanden is marked on old OS maps as a detached fragment of Leigh Parish. From Hollanden, the last mile and a half continues along the forest pale of the North Frith hunting forest to Somegate.

Start at the church entrance in Underriver and pass the church and Old Vicarage on your left, then turn left along a restricted by-way passing houses on your left. Continue through a kissing gate into a field and go along the left side and through into the next field. Veer left through a line of oak trees to the left  corner and go over a stile. Continue along the left side of the next field through an oak avenue to a gate. Go through, then over a stile and then through another gate and continue along the left side of the field to the next corner. Cross a stile to a road (Underriver House Road).

The by-way was clearly once a wide lane or drove and a direct route between Shipbourne and Underriver.

Turn right and go along the road for about a quarter of a mile, then turn left over a stile, just before a house called Hollandhurst. Bear left across the field towards a stile in the next hedge. Go over and cross the field keeping near to the right hedge and going towards the right side of a row of houses. Join a paddock fence on your right for a while, turn right over a stile, cross the paddock and go over another stile. Cross a footbridge and turn left along a track, passing Grenadier Cottages. Continue to Riding Lane.

The houses are named after a pub called 'The Grenadier' which is marked on late 19th century maps but was flattened by a bomb in 1942. This area is just within the old detached part of Leigh Parish called Hollanden. At the other side of Riding Lane, the Tonbridge forest of North Frith begins.

Turn right and continue along Riding Lane passing Gardener's Hope Cottages on your right. Soon turn left at a footpath sign along a tarmac drive to Fairhill. Go across a bridge and follow the drive between laurel hedges passing the entrance to Fairhill. As the drive bears left continue directly ahead, over a stile and then uphill through woods (bluebells in the spring). At the end of the wood, go over a stile onto an enclosed path next to a field. Notice the bank on your left.

The 13th century forest pale and the Tonbridge boundary followed (and still does) the left side of the footpath and it is an obvious boundary whether a bank or mature hedge. You are walking as the jurors did, 'and so by the pale of the forest'

Continue along the enclosed path, go over a stile, cross a track and go forward across a bridge to a green metal gate by a stile. Go over the stile and continue along an enclosed path. Cross another stile and continue through a wood where the boundary bank appears again and the footpath will go over it. Come out of the wood to a field and continue alongside the left hedge. Tinley Lodge Farm is over on the right. Go through a gate and continue ahead to a farm drive. Turn left, pass a new house on your right and then turn right into a wood. Continue along an enclosed path.

Eventually bear right round a cypressus hedge, cross a drive and instead of going straight on, veer left in front of a wooden field gate and follow an enclosed path between fields to a hedge. Go through to Hildenborough Road. Cross over and turn right along a wide grass verge.

According to Hasted's maps 'Somegate,' the start and finish of the perambulation seems to be here in the area of West Green Farm. It is difficult to be more precise than this with the name now lost.

Shortly turn left over a footbridge and go directly across a field to a yellow painted post at the corner of a wood. Continue alongside the wood on your left to the corner. Keep directly ahead across the field and turn right at a stream on a path leading uphill to the church. Aim for a yellow post on the far side of the field and turn left here following a hedge on your right. Come to a small stand of trees and at the field corner turn right through a kissing gate into the church yard. Follow the church round and continue to the lych gate to emerge on Stumble Hill at Shipbourne at the end of the perambulation (33 miles)! Turn right for the Chaser Inn.

St Giles Church in Shipbourne was built in 1879 by Edward Cazalet of Fairlawn although there has been a church on the site since mediaeval times. Constructed of ragstone, the lichen has given it an interesting red hue.

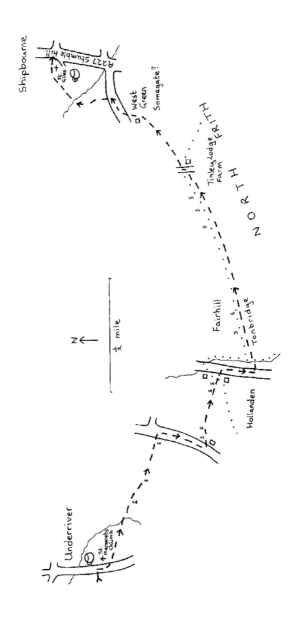

Tonbridge Castle to Ford Green Bridge

Maps:	OS Explorer 136
Distance:	4 miles (circular; 9 miles)
Stiles:	1 stile
Start:	Tonbridge Castle
Parking:	Tonbridge
Refresh:	Cafes, Shops and Pubs; Tonbridge

Tonbridge Castle is the centre of the lowy of Tonbridge. It is from here that the lowy was planned, established, maintained and preserved, so that it survived as the basis of Tonbridge Parish in the 19th century. The castle is well worth a visit to see the kind of institution and the characters that were at the heart of Tonbridge and first put it on the map as a place of significance in mediaeval England.

This walk is the east link from Tonbridge Castle to the route of the 13th century perambulation at Ford Green Bridge, via the Medway Valley. It follows the Weald Way (WW) throughout. Included are directions for a different route back to Tonbridge via Postern, one of the Clares' Parks.

Start

Start at the top of the motte, go down the spiral path, turn right at the bottom and go directly ahead to the river. Turn left and continue with the river on your right to the High Street. Turn right across the bridge and soon turn left along Medway Wharf Road. Join the south bank of the river on your left, pass Town Lock and continue passing apartment blocks on your right. Arrive at Vale Road and turn left across Cannon Bridge.

Cross over the road (now Cannon Lane), turn right for a few paces and then turn left along a footpath (WW) following the north bank of the river. Continue to a farm road bridge. Go under the bridge, pass a pillbox on your left and go through a gap by the side of a field gate. Continue along the bank and cross a footbridge.

To the left you will see houses and farm buildings on a low hill. This is Hadlow Stair which was a landing place on the river in mediaeval times. The route to Hadlow from Tonbridge (now Old Hadlow Road) used to pass through here and so had a very winding course.

Arrive at Eldridge's Lock and continue through fields. Cross a footbridge and continue with woodland on your left. Pass Porters Lock and on your left some scrubby wood and a pill box. Cross a footbridge and arrive at Hartlake Bridge. Go under the bridge and continue along the north bank.

Hartlake Bridge was the scene of a terrible tragedy on 20th October 1853. About 30 hop pickers drowned, when the wooden bridge collapsed under their horse drawn wagon.

On the left is the small hamlet of Hartlake. There are good views of Hadlow Tower and soon Golden Green will appear on the ridge to the left. Beyond Golden Green on the far greensand ridge you may see the church of St Michael's, East Peckham.

At East Lock, pass two pill boxes on your left and a green metal fence on your right. Go right over the footbridge and then up and down a small flight of steps. Cross over the lock to the south bank. Turn left and go through a kissing gate and continue ahead along the south bank of the river. Arrive at Ford Green Bridge and go through a kissing gate to the bridge. If you wish to continue on the 13th century walk round Tonbridge in a clockwise direction, go to page 27.

Return to Tonbridge via Postern

At the bridge, go straight through another kissing gate and turn right in the direction of Five Oak Green. Go along the right side of a field and come to a wood on the right. Veer right into the wood (about 100 metres before the end of the field) and continue to a stile. Go over the stile and cross a footbridge. Continue ahead to a lake and follow an enclosed path with the lake on your left until you come to a hedge. Go through and cross a footbridge to a smaller lake. Turn left and continue following the fence round until you arrive at a wooden railed footbridge on your left.

Cross the footbridge and continue ahead to where the path forks (just before the oak trees). Pass right of the first oak tree and bear right across the field, continuing towards a broken line of oak trees. Join a stream and follow it on your left then cross it over a concrete bridge.

Bear right to a field corner, cross a footbridge and continue along the left side of the next field. Pass woodland on your right and cross another field, still following the left hedge. Bear right with the hedge for a short distance and cross a footbridge on your left into the next field. Continue to a path junction in the middle of the field.

Turn right, go through a gap in the next hedge and head directly across the next field to a footbridge. Cross over, continue across another field and go through a gap. Go across the next field, cross a footbridge and then continue ahead between currant bushes along a grassy path. Arrive at a ditch and turn left, keeping the ditch on your right and fruit bushes on the left. Go into the next field continuing along a stony track. Pass a pylon on your left and head for farm buildings. At Sherenden Farm, cross the yard with the buildings on your right and go through a gap at the side of a metal gate. Continue along Sherenden Road with the farm buildings on your right. Go past Sherenden Farm cottages on your left and Latters Farm cottages on your right to a road (Hartlake Road).

Turn right and just after Hale Farm Cottages, turn left along a drive. Turn right in front of a wooden telegraph pole. Go across the field towards a hedge corner and then continue alongside the hedge on your right. At the field corner, go over a small plank footbridge into the next field. Go slightly left aiming for a way-marked post on the far side. Turn left at the post and continue along the right side of the field to a path junction. Turn right, cross a footbridge and continue alongside a hedge on your left.

This is Postern Park in which the Clares used to keep deer for release into the South Frith hunting forest to the left and uphill. It was probably chosen because it was close to the castle, dry and had good access to the forest. The hedge on your left is long and straight and was probably the edge of the park.

By the 17th century the parks were divided into farms and hops were grown. On the right there is an interesting variety of oasts.

Come to a point where the left hedge has shifted to the right and following way-marks go through, continuing with the hedge on your right. At the next field corner go through a kissing gate into an orchard. Continue ahead to another corner and go through a gate into a minor lane. Turn left and come to Postern Lane. Turn right and pass the 'Postern' on your right (possibly the original entrance to the park).

The road is now on a high causeway with Postern Forge on your right. Continue along the road ascending to Postern Heath, then go downhill to Postern Bridge which spans the Botany Stream (one of the Medway channels of which there used to be five). The river Medway comes closer in on the right as you approach Cannon Bridge. Arrive at Cannon Bridge and turn right over the bridge, then cross over Cannon Lane at the island and turn left, back across the bridge. Turn right just after the bridge along the riverside footpath and continue along the river to Town Lock. Turn left onto Medway Wharf Road and continue along it to the High Street and Tonbridge Castle.

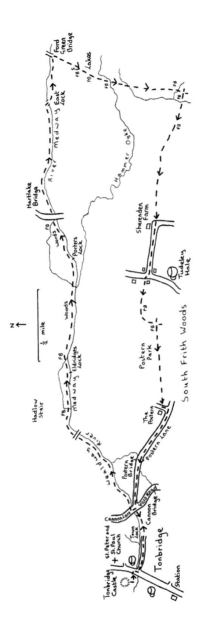

80

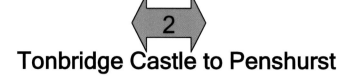

Tonbridge Castle to Penshurst

Maps:	OS Explorer 147
Distance:	5 miles
Stiles:	5 stiles
Start:	Tonbridge Castle
Parking:	Tonbridge
Refresh:	Cafes, Shops and Pubs; Tonbridge and Penshurst

This walk links Tonbridge Castle with Penshurst, two significant places in 13th century Tonbridge. The castle was the centre of the lowy and home of the Clares. Penshurst was the home of Lord Stephen of Penshurst, knight, who held most of the land between Tonbridge and Penshurst and who presided over the perambulation at Tonbridge Castle, as a justice. His estate remains, but not his home which was replaced by a magnificent hall house in the 14th century. His effigy is in Penshurst Church lying unceremoniously on the floor

This walk is the west link from Tonbridge to the 13th century perambulation route at Penshurst via the Medway Valley. It follows the Eden Valley Walk (EVW) throughout.

Start at the top of the motte, go down the spiral path, turn right at the bottom and go directly ahead to the river. Turn right (EVW) and follow the motte on your right then turn left to the entrance of the swimming pool. Turn right and continue with the miniature railway on your left. When you come to the road, go across to the right side of the Tonbridge Juddians Rugby Club and proceed along a footpath following a stream on your right (Hilden Brook). Continue between sports fields with a hedge on your left and stream on your right and cross a footbridge. Continue ahead through sports fields and soon the path will be joined by a cycle track. Keep straight on and go under the railway and continue through a wooded area to join the river Medway. Turn right and cross a footbridge.

Here the river is wide with islands and on the opposite bank is Barden Park, once a large country house owned by the Judd family and now a housing estate. In Norman times it was a significant place with its own church (now lost) and possibly a fishery.

Continue along the river on a track shared with cyclists. Turn left over a footbridge signed Haysden Country Park and cross another footbridge. Continue ahead with the river on your left and arrive at Lucifer Bridge. This is a good alternative route in very muddy conditions and will take you round Barden Lake (consult maps), otherwise continue on the right side of the river. Keep straight ahead through fields and woodland with the river on your left and eventually arrive at a metal railed footbridge on your left called 'Friendship Bridge.' Cross the bridge, turn right and continue to a wooden field gate with a sign to the 'Flood Barrier,' but don't go through.

This was the site of an old weir that used to be called 'the lido' and was a favourite bathing area. It was filled in when the flood barrier was built to regulate river flow after the floods of 1968. It is now a plantation with trees donated by Tonbridge's twin town Heusenstamm, Germany.

Turn left in front of the gate and continue, going under a railway arch. Come out by 'Rainbow Bridge' and continue directly ahead through a gap and then over 'Straight Mile Bridge.' Turn right, continuing with the EVW. Follow a straight causeway between two parallel channels.

This 'straight mile' was an attempt in about 1830 to dig canals at least as far as Penshurst. James Christie whose brainchild it was became bankrupt and fled to America and the scheme was never finished. A huge amount of excavation was involved as you can see

Arrive at the flood barrier and the A21, Tonbridge By-Pass.

The flood barrier was another massive earthwork constructed here in 1978 as a response to the frequent and serious floods overwhelming Tonbridge, especially in 1968. In prolonged periods of heavy rain the valley upstream of the barrier is allowed to flood, creating a lake. Water is then slowly released so that sudden flooding is prevented in Tonbridge.

Go up the barrier, turn left and go under the A21 road bridge. Turn right down the barrier and reach a lakeside (Haysden Water). Continue round the lake (keeping it on your left) and keep to the path, eventually crossing the 'James Christie Bridge.' Turn right and go along another section of the 'Straight Mile' until you come to a path junction with a post in the middle.

Go straight on and soon you will notice the river coming nearer to the footpath. Bear left and then right along the footpath which is now at a higher level. Go through a gap to Ensfield Road and turn right over the road bridge. After the bridge turn left through a stile and follow the north bank of the Medway.

(An alternative in wet weather and muddy conditions is to continue along Ensfield Road and take a later left turn along the paved cycle track to Penshurst). Keep alongside the river and go through a wide gap in a field hedge. Shortly turn right at a footpath sign (on a tree), go across the field towards a wooden footbridge and cross over.

Bear left uphill to a stile in the fence. Go through to a drive (Killicks Bank) and turn right to the paved track which is also the cycle route. Turn left and go uphill with good views of Tonbridge behind and Ashour Woods to the left. When the track bears left to Well Place keep directly ahead, still following the EVW. You will soon reach a metal gate with stile and a view of Penshurst Place below. Go through and continue downhill, across the field to another stile in the next hedge. Go through and follow the left hedge of the next field until you reach a stile about half way along. Go through to the road, turn right and pass lakes on your right. Eventually you will pass Penshurst Place on your right and arrive at the entrance arch which leads to the village. If you wish to continue on the 13th century walk round Tonbridge in a clockwise direction, go to page 55.

Penshurst is worth exploring and is full of delights. Penshurst Place has a fine example of a 14th century hall and imaginative gardens. It has long been the home of the Sidney family, who were once Earls of Leicester, now the Viscounts de Lisle.

If you are returning back to Tonbridge, retracing your steps is the best way to avoid roads and the views are glorious.

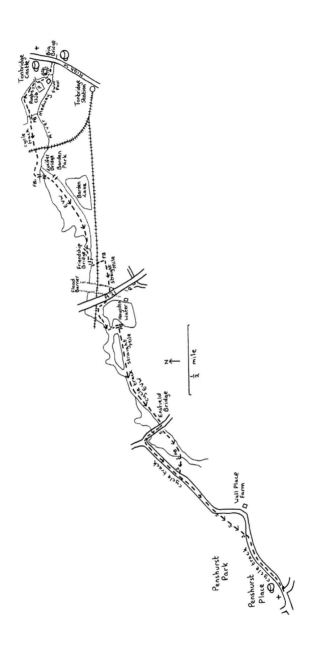

85

Shipbourne and the Bourne Valley

Maps:	OS Explorer 147, 148
Distance:	5 miles
Stiles:	6 stiles
Start:	The Chaser Inn; TQ 593523
Parking:	Shipbourne Green
Refresh:	The Chaser Inn, Shipbourne;
	Kentish Rifleman, Dunks Gr.

This walk is gentle and full of variety, through coppiced woodland and large arable fields with good views across the Bourne Valley. The perambulation begins with the large northern hunting forest of Tonbridge, 'the North Frith' bounded in 1279 with park pales and hedges.

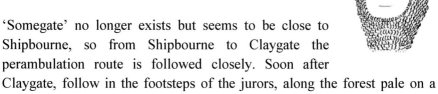

'The jury..began the lowy at Somegate..in the parish of Tonbridge and so along the hedges and pale including the northern forest to Claygate and so to Larkhale..'

'Somegate' no longer exists but seems to be close to Shipbourne, so from Shipbourne to Claygate the perambulation route is followed closely. Soon after Claygate, follow in the footsteps of the jurors, along the forest pale on a high boundary bank through woods on the edge of North Frith.

Start

Start at The Chaser Inn and cross the road (Stumble Hill) to the Common so that you are on the same side of the road as the red telephone box. In between the first two trees, look for a grassy footpath (not signed but marked on the OS Map) that bears left across the Common. Follow the path, passing right of a large oak tree and towards a line of trees. Keep the trees on your right for a while and you will come to a path junction. Look right for a gate set back in the trees, go through it and cross a field to Back Lane. Turn left along the lane, then right along Reeds Lane.

The Tonbridge forest of North Frith rose uphill on the right as it does today, but probably extended nearer to the lanes.

Pass 'Martins' on your right and then turn right along a byway until you reach a lane. Turn right here to Claygate.

Claygate was an entrance into the North Frith forest. Long before the Normans this ancient road was used by Wrotham folk for access to the forest and the Medway valley.

At the T junction, turn right along Puttenden Road and continue across a bridge over the Bourne and uphill passing houses on your left. Just beyond 'Hookwood' (the third house) turn left through woods at a footpath sign. Continue to a way-marked path junction.

Note the boundary stone on the left. From here, Hadlow Parish (once part of the lowy of Tonbridge) is on your right and West Peckham on your left.

87

Go directly ahead along the top of the boundary bank.

This bank was probably the line of the forest pale and the exact route of the perambulation. In the 13th century Hadlow and the 'North Frith' were both part of the lowy of Tonbridge. On the West Peckham side, Clearhedges was outside the lowy, although the Clares had tried to possess it.

Continue along the bank until you arrive at a junction with a wide track. Turn right and then left following signs. Descend through the wood and eventually turn right into a field, then continue alongside the edge of the wood and then a hedge. Go through a gap into the next field and continue towards a belt of trees ahead. Turn right just before and continue with the trees on your left until you emerge on High House Lane at Stallions Green. Turn left, pass a bungalow on your left and continue along the winding lane until you come to a house on the left called Mount Pleasant.

High House Lane from Stallions Green to Mount Pleasant follows the eastern edge of the mediaeval North Frith Park. At Mount Pleasant the north east corner of the park is reached. It could be the site of 'Larkhale' of the perambulation after which there is no more mention of a forest. The word 'hale' suggests corner or raised area of land surrounded by watery meadows and Mount Pleasant on a corner of the Bourne, fits both these descriptions.

Turn left along the track just beyond Mount Pleasant and shortly cross a stile on the right, opposite a gate. Go through rough pasture to a line of trees on the right, joining the river Bourne. Continue through a large field alongside the river on your right.

The Bourne, the field on the left and the woods beyond are all in the area of Clearhedges, West Peckham. It is good fertile land and with the mills along the Bourne it is easy to understand why the Clares desired it. On the other side of the stream are the buildings of old Oxenhoath Mill. This and the mill on Hamptons Lane (shortly reached on the walk) were taken by the Clares, but were returned.

As you approach the end of the field, look for a footbridge with a metal rail on your right (opposite a wide footpath leading across the field to the left). Cross over and then turn left through a field with a pylon. Go directly ahead towards a field gate and cross the stile to Hamptons Lane. Turn left passing the Fish Farm on your right (*the site of a fulling mill in the 13th century*). Continue up the lane and just before a house on your right, turn right into a drive and continue ahead along a grassy footpath which becomes enclosed. After about 300 metres, go through a kissing gate in the left fence and cross the field to emerge on Dunks Green Road.

For the 'Kentish Rifleman' Pub; turn right and then right again.

Cross the road to a footpath opposite, up stone steps. Go through the gate and go along the left side of the field looking out for a stile on your left. Turn left over the stile and bear right across the field to a wood. Go over another stile, cross a small stream and continue up through the wood until you come to a path junction. Look for a field gate ahead and slightly to the right. At the gate, go over the stile and head directly across the field to another stile and emerge at School Lane. Cross over and follow the drive through Fairlawn Home Farm. Pass the farm buildings on your right and continue directly ahead along a track going downhill and then up towards houses. At the houses, bear left and go through a gate to an enclosed track that brings you out at Shipbourne Common. Turn right for The Chaser Inn.

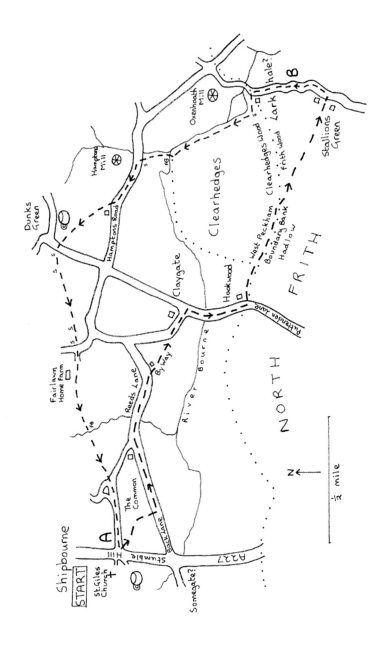

90

2 Hadlow and the Common

Maps:	OS Explorer 136, 148
Distance:	3 miles
Stiles:	5 stiles
Start:	Hadlow Square; TQ 634497
Transport:	Bus 7, Tonbridge to Hadlow
Parking:	Hadlow Village
Refresh:	Pubs and shops, Hadlow

In this walk the North Frith forest with its park pales and hedges are left behind to be replaced by the mills, meadows, and large arable fields of the Bourne Valley. Hadlow Tower and Church are well worth visiting (check websites for opening times).

'..and so from Larkhale...through the midst of Lomewood..'

Although these names are not used today, Larkhale and Lomewood existed recently enough to locate them; in fact Lomewood is still present in a street name and is the former name for Hadlow Common.

The church contains some old, possibly Saxon features; the fabric however, is mainly mediaeval (open most afternoons from 2 to 4pm).

Start where Church Street joins Hadlow Square with your back to the church. Turn left and cross over the A26 aiming for a narrow street between Lime Tree House and Hadlow Post Office called School Lane. Proceed along this street passing the Library on your right and Scout HQ on your left. Cross Hailstone Road and continue ahead until you come out at Carpenters Lane. Turn right passing 'The Rose & Crown' and just after 'Mill View,' go left at a footpath sign down a lane to Bourne Mill.

Bourne Mill was working as a corn mill until 1947 when it was taken over by Mr Carr as a small clothing factory. It is still trading today as Carr and Westley.

Cross the car park to a footbridge ahead, cross over and continue over another footbridge. Bear right and follow an enclosed path with a field on your left. At the end of the field, go through a woody patch and cross a stile on your left into the next field. Continue along the right side of the field and go over a stile at a field gate. Cross another stile on your left by a similar gate. Follow the line of willows on your left and go under overhead power cables. Look out for a way-marked post on your left. Turn right here and go across the field, and then across the next field. Arrive at a stile and cross to High House Lane, Stallions Green. Turn right and pass a bungalow on your left, looking out for the next footpath on your right.

Turn right over a stile by a field gate, and follow the right hedge to the river Bourne. Cross a footbridge, go across a meadow and through the next hedge. Over to the right marked by a clump of trees, is the site of a moat. Continue towards the left side of it.

The story of this moat is not known but moats were commonly dug around houses in the 13th and 14th centuries, so it is likely there was a house here in 1279. A spring higher up the hill is connected with the site and might have supplied clean water. The house by the spring could have replaced the moat house when they became less fashionable or desirable.

From the moat continue along the footpath in the same direction as you arrived, going gradually uphill through the large field to the far left corner. Hadlow Tower will appear ahead. At the field corner, go through a kissing gate to a road (Carpenters Lane) at Steers Place.

There is a road sign here to The Common; called Hadlow Common, it is the 'Lomewood' of the perambulation.

Cross Carpenters Lane and go ahead along Steers Place (a winding lane) in the direction of The Common. Arrive at a T junction (Common Road) and turn right along the road.

 *The Common 'lomewood' was on both sides of the road, so that as the jurors did in 1279, you are walking through the 'midst of lomewood.'*

Continue past Laxton Farm on your left and when you reach footpath signs, turn right along an enclosed path and eventually reach a road. Turn left and continue to the Maidstone Road (A26). Turn right and continue to Cemetery Lane on your left just before 'The Harrow.'

Close to this junction there was once a cross called Durrants Cross offering protection for travellers walking from the village of Hadlow as they left the safety of their houses and entered Lomewood or the Common.

More than once the cemetery on Cemetery Lane was thought to be a good site for burials as two Romano/British cremations (2,000 years old) were discovered there in the late 19th Century.

The late W.V. Dumbreck is buried there. An eminent Hadlow historian, in 1958 he translated and published part of the 1279 perambulation document in 'Archaeologia Cantiana.' It was an important source for this project.

Pass 'The Harrow' on your left, and then continue to the village square.

The stretch of water on your left is a stream which used to flow down the street from the Common and frequently flood the centre of Hadlow.

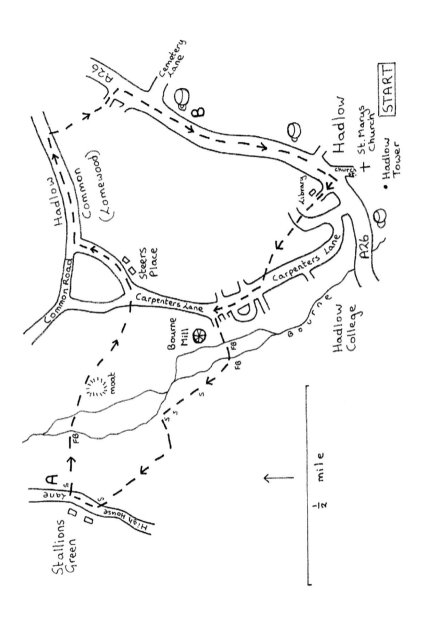

© Crown copyright 2013 Ordnance Survey 100054134

3 Hadlow and Golden Green

Maps:	OS Explorer 136, 148
Distance:	4.5 miles
Stiles:	1 stile
Start:	Hadlow Square; TQ 634497
Transport:	Bus 7, Tonbridge to Hadlow
Parking:	Hadlow Village
Refresh:	Pubs and shops, Hadlow;
	The Bell. Golden Green

On this walk you pass the mills, meadows, orchards and large arable fields of the Bourne valley. Hadlow Tower is often visible as the circular walk skirts round it. Hadlow Tower and Church are worth a visit (check websites for opening times).

'..to the domus of Peter Fromund..to the Kings Highway which includes the land of Hugo de Waldis and..to the messuage of Pepin and so directly over the field to the hall of Peter de la Mare...'

A series of tenants are listed whose lands or houses the perambulation passes. A third of all properties are in this section. The Hadlow boundary zigzags wildly in now empty fields, but at the time it skirted round and sometimes through individual tenements.

Start

At the end of Church Street on the village square with your back to the church, turn right and continue along the Maidstone Road eventually passing a stretch of water on the right. Just before a row of cottages turn right along a footpath to East Peckham.

Follow the enclosed path to a field, cross to the next hedge and go over a footbridge. Go across the next field and then zigzag with the path around field hedges on your left, looking for a concealed way-marked post by a left turn through a straight section of hedge. Go through the hedge and you will see an orchard on the left and a high silver birch hedge on the right. Turn  right and go round the hedge and then continue alongside it with a smaller hedge on your right. Continue through the next field and on to a kissing gate in a high hedge ahead of you.

Go through to Cemetery Lane, turn left and then immediately right into Goblands Farm (now a small industrial estate). Turn next left towards a black painted clapboard building called 'Hoppers,' then turn right along a track passing buildings on your right. At the end go left and then right after a small group of painted containers. Follow a grassy track ahead between fields and about 100 metres short of a wood bear left across a field and then continue on a grassy track through the wood.

This wood is on the Hadlow Parish boundary and the jurors probably came this way. It is here that a number of tenements or lands belonging to different owners were passed. Some of the fields are called 'bounds fields' and a part belonged to Peter Fromund who is named on the perambulation.

The 'beating of the bounds' which took place during Rogationtide (usually in May) zigzagged round these fields and crossed over stiles. One such stile was known as 'the cider stile' where the Goding family (later the Golding family of Golding Hop fame) offered the bound beaters a pail of cider.

Come out of the wood to a path junction. Turn right and then bear left across a large field towards another wood. At the end of the field turn right and then right again through the same field on another trajectory. Cross a stile into a sports ground and go across towards two wooden posts, marking a gap in the hedge. Go through and emerge on Bells Farm Lane. Turn right following the parish boundary along the lane.

There is reason to think that this road is the 'Kings Highway' of the perambulation since the boundary follows the road and therefore it is likely the road is as old. There are very few places around Tonbridge where roads are aligned with parish boundaries.

Continue along the lane passing Bells Farmhouse on your left. Shortly join Court Lane coming in from the right and keep ahead. Soon you will come to a three way junction at Kent House Farm.

The 'Kings Highway' is said in the perambulation to include the lands of Hugo de Waldis (Weald). The suggestion is that while his lands were within, his house was not. The name Kent House Farm is interesting because there are other Kent Farms or Kent Houses on the boundary of the lowy. Anyone leaving the lowy left the special jurisdiction of Tonbridge (under the Earl) and entered the different jurisdiction of Kent (under the Sheriff). Hugo's house could have been the 'Kent House' on Kent House Farm.

From the junction continue ahead along Pierce Mill Lane. There is little traffic on this lane but watch out for cyclists coming fast round the bends.

Across the fields to the right and concealed by trees is Caxton Place, tentatively linked to the first English printer, William Caxton. He was born and brought up in the weald of Kent. The farm became Simmons brewery in 1830 which operated until 1905. To provide clean water an artesian well about 860 ft deep was cut into the aquifer. Now it feeds winter storage reservoirs for irrigating salad crops grown in the surrounding fields.

When you arrive at the old mill workshop on the left, look out on your right for a footpath sign (Weald Way), concealed in the hedge. Go through a gate into a small yard and keep straight ahead following the signs. Go through to a gravel drive and veer left to a grassy bank on the other side. Continue alongside a row of concrete mushrooms, following the river Bourne on your left. Soon leave the garden and the path becomes quite overgrown as it goes through scrubby woodland. Eventually pass a way-marked post and come out into the corner of a large arable field. Go along the left side of this field passing a footbridge on your left.

Continue alongside the river Bourne on your left for some distance. Eventually you will come to Victoria Road and if you would like a refreshment stop, turn left here for 'The Bell Inn' at Golden Green.

Golden Green is on a prominent ridge between the Bourne and Medway rivers. This dry situation between rivers has attracted settlement from prehistoric times and the name Goldhill could relate to gold coins or other treasures found here. The rivers were well used for milling, meadows, fisheries and transport. Hadlow had 12 fisheries in 1086, and several mills. In the late 18th Century Hasted remarked "near the river the grasslands are very rich, capable of fatting beasts of a large size" (Vol. 5 p.177). Improved drainage has now reclaimed the meadows for arable crops.

Cross Victoria Road and continue along the south (left) bank of the Bourne. Soon turn right across a footbridge to follow the north bank again.

From the footbridge you can see Goldhill Mill further along the south side. It was a corn mill and most of the milling machinery is still intact. The site has now been developed for holiday cottages.

Turn left and continue following the river until you come to a T junction. Turn right and follow the wooden fence on your left. At the end of the fence enter a large field and turn left following the field edge round. Eventually you will come to a way-marked post. Go left here into a wood along an unpromising narrow track. Continue going uphill through woodland. Arrive at a post in about 200 metres, where you turn left off the woodland track and into Hadlow College land.

Go through a kissing gate into a large field and Hadlow tower is very prominent ahead. Continue ahead on the Hadlow Access Trail where the paths are paved and there are occasional benches. At the end of the field go through a kissing gate then follow a fence on your left to a path junction. Keep left and come alongside the backs of gardens. Come out into a modern estate road and notice the imposing gate posts on the left.

This is the site of Hadlow Castle which was demolished in 1952 leaving just the tower, entrance gate and some outbuildings. The tower was built as a folly in 1840 to complete the gothic mansion. It was saved from demolition by Bernard Hailstone, the war artist.

Bear left to a T junction and continue ahead along a path between houses. Pass St Marys Church on your left and turn right along Church Street to Hadlow Square.

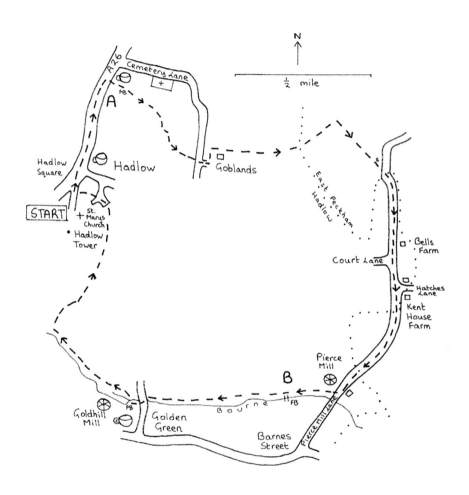

N

½ mile

A26
Cemetery Lane
FB
A
Hadlow Square
Hadlow
Goblands
East Peckham Hadlow
START
St. Marys Church
• Hadlow Tower
Court Lane
Bells Farm
Hatches Lane
Kent House Farm
Pierce Mill
B
Bourne
FB
FB
Goldhill Mill
Golden Green
Barnes Street
Pierce Mill Lane

Maps:	OS Explorer 136
Distance:	✓ 5 miles
Stiles:	3 stiles
Start:	Car Park, Kelchers Lane; TQ 639483
Transport:	Bus 208, Tonbridge/Golden Green
Parking:	Car Park (small), Kelchers Lane
Refresh:	The Bell, Golden Green
	Pubs and shop, Five Oak Green

The Medway Valley is a low, flat country of lakes, streams, ditches and large unenclosed fields under huge skies. In the 13th century the nutritious meadows were used for fattening stock in drier seasons and the watercourses and river for fishing and ferrying.

'to the mill of John Curtone..so all the tenements of the Prior and of the Archbishop of Canterbury be without and so to Cnokewerespole and from there to wynelingbroke..'

The mill of John de Curtone may be Little Mill just to the east of Barnes Street. 'Cnokewerespole' translates as Oak Weir Pool and there is an Oak Weir Lock today where the perambulation crossed the Medway.

Start

Start in the small car park at the entrance to Kelchers Lane in Golden Green (from Tonbridge it is just beyond 'The Bell Inn' and on the right). Cross the road and turn right along Three Elm Lane (divert along Medway View to get off the road for a short while). Continue to No. 21 and then turn left along a grassy footpath and go through a gate. Go on a right diagonal across the field and at the corner, cross over a small stream into another field and bear left going alongside the Bourne. Continue to a metal railed footbridge on your left (don't cross).

Turn right across the same field (along the 'Weald Way' WW) to a field hedge. Officially, the footpath passes through the hedge and rejoins the field further round but if it is blocked or the route is unclear, turn left and continue alongside the hedge on your right. Whichever way you go, you will follow eventually, a stream and an old stone and brick wall on your right. Arrive at a gate with a gap on the left and go through to Barnes Street. Barnes Place is opposite and Poplar Court on the right.

There are some picturesque buildings in Barnes Street of mediaeval origin. Part of Barnes Place is a two bay hall house possibly dating to the 13th century. The earl of Gloucester made grants of lands in return for military service or rent. Poplar Court has an early 16th century cross wing.

The route of the 1279 perambulation is about a quarter of a mile to the east (left) as it followed the boundary of Hadlow and East Peckham. This walk to Five Oak Green just inside the boundary is better served with footpaths.

again

Cross the road (Three Elm Lane) to Barnes Place, turn right (WW) and then left along a track. Go over a stile and continue past a hay barn on your left. Turn left after the barn and go towards the entrance of a farm yard. *but* Just before, turn right through a metal gate and join a footpath with a line of beech trees on the right and a stream on the left. Continue and go through a gate keeping alongside the stream on your left. Go straight on through another gate and across the next field. Cross a third field, go through a gate to Ford Green Bridge and cross over the river Medway.

Oak Weir Lock, the 'cnokewerespole' of the perambulation is about half a mile downstream from here. It is not well served with footpaths and so is Miss Out *not included on this walk but it can be visited by turning left after the bridge and then returning to this point (30 minutes in total).*

N/A Tonbridge (4 miles) can be reached from here by turning right after the bridge and following the Weald Way (see Link Walk 1).

Once over the bridge, go through a kissing gate on your left and then turn right in the direction of Five Oak Green. Go along the right side of the field and before the end, veer right into a wood and continue to a stile. Go over the stile, cross a footbridge and continue

forward to a lake. Keeping the lake on your left, continue along an enclosed path to a hedge. Go through and cross a footbridge to a smaller lake. Turn left and follow the fence round to the other side of the lake until you arrive at a wooden railed footbridge on your left.

This remote area is uninhabited and is left for fishing, agriculture and gravel works (now bird sanctuaries). The remoteness made it a good place to set up a starfish bombing decoy in May 1942, where controlled fires deflected bombers from Tonbridge.

The footbridge crosses Hammer Dyke which is the boundary between Hadlow and Capel Parishes. Part of Capel was connected to the Manor of Hadlow and was therefore in the lowy of Tonbridge.

Ahead, you can see a forested ridge. This upland area is the great 'South Frith' forest; another great hunting park of the Earl's to match that of the North Frith.

Junction of Figure of 8.

Cross the footbridge and then in about 100 metres (just before the oak trees) the footpath forks. Turn left here so that the first oak tree is on your right. Continue and some oasts (Moat Farm) will come into view. As you approach Moat Farm turn left and then right over a footbridge. Turn left right keeping the farm buildings and fence on your right.

Moat Farm had mediaeval origins and in among the modern industrial units there is an old farmhouse. It is on a slight hill and so for the first time since Barnes Street the land is dry enough to build on.

At the fence corner, turn right keeping the farm buildings on your right and orchards on your left. Cross over a drive and go through a gap in the hedge. Kissing gate. Turn right and continue alongside the hedge on your right and when you begin to turn away from the farm buildings, look out for a gap in the tall hedge on your right.

Go through the gap and cross a footbridge to the farm drive. Turn left and continue along to the junction with Whetsted Road. Turn right, go over the railway bridge and continue to the road junction at Five Oak Green.

Turn right along Five Oak Green Road passing an iron chapel on your right and then 'The Hoppers' (not a pub).

'The Hoppers' began life as a row of 18th century cottages and then became a hoppers' pub called the 'Rose & Crown.' Father Richard Wilson from Stepney followed his parishioners on a hop picking season and was appalled by the squalor and drunken state in which many of them lived. He started a temperance campaign and in 1906 bought the pub, and converted it into a hospital for children with a games room and a sheltered courtyard with two fireplaces where the hoppers could socialise. Now it is used as a holiday home or retreat for East London charities and churches.

Continue along Five Oak Green Road and cross Oak Road.

Notice the names Brooklands and Brookdene opposite the entrance to Oak Road. 'Brook' is often found in names over a large area on the other side of the road; perhaps the 'wynelingbroke' of the perambulation. The Alder stream meanders on a very winding course through Capel and Five Oak Green on its way to the Medway.

Cross Larkfield and continue for about 300 metres. Turn right at a footpath sign (opposite Sychem Lane) and continue along a tarmac drive for about 400 metres to Finches Farm. Turn left in front of a farm building and arrive at an area of hoppers huts with the cook houses still intact.

Pass the huts on your right and then bear right towards a railway bridge. Go

 under the railway and continue ahead along the track which crosses a field. Arrive at a gate, go through and continue to a path junction in the middle of the field.

Continue ahead, go over a wide bridge to another field and follow the right hedge. Keep alongside the right hedge passing a wood on your left. Cross another field and then go over a footbridge and a stile to the next field. Go straight on and cross a wide footbridge over a ditch. Bear right following the ditch on your right and continue towards an oak tree. Keep straight on and go over the footbridge. Continue ahead between two lakes. *Same oaks*

(Hammer Dyke) *as page 105*

Cross a footbridge and go across the middle of a field. Go over another footbridge, cross another field and then a short field to a kissing gate at East Lock. Go through and cross over the lock, then turn left to cross another bridge over a canoe weir and then a third bridge to the opposite bank. Turn left and then right between two pill boxes and follow a good track towards Golden Green. When the track bears left keep ahead along a footpath passing left of an oak tree. Cross another field heading for the right side of a line of poplars. When you reach the poplars continue ahead with the poplar windbreak now on your left. Continue to a kissing gate and go through to Kelchers Lane. Continue to the car park and Golden Green.

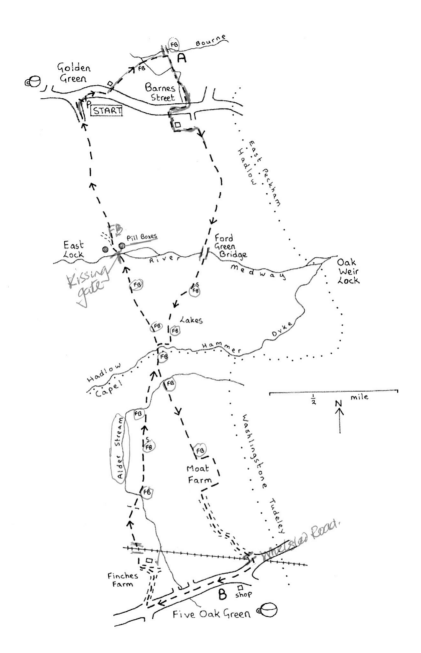

108

5 Five Oak Green and Capel

Maps:	OS Explorer 136
Distance:	4.5 miles (5 miles including church)
Stiles:	11 stiles
Start:	Village Shop; TQ 648454
Transport:	Bus 205 Tonbridge/Five Oak Green.
Parking:	Car park, Falmouth Place.
Refresh:	Pubs and shop, Five Oak Green.
	The Dovecote, Alders Road.

This walk follows the Alder Stream upstream to the old forest of Tonbridge, the 'South Frith'. The hills of Pembury and Capel are covered with apple orchards and the woodland around Old Pembury is carpeted with bluebells and wild garlic in spring. Visit the 13th century wall paintings in Capel Church.

'wynelingbroke is within..and so by the highway to Dodingebury which is without..the tenements of Wechelstone and Brenchesle are without..so west as far as the pale of the forest..'

The *'wynelingbroke'* is a 'winding' brook such as the Alder Stream flowing through Five Oak Green on its way to the Medway (where there are many 'brook' names). On the way to the forest pale at Old Pembury you will pass through Washlingstone hundred and 'Dodingebury,' now Downingbury.

Start

Facing the shop at Five Oak Green, turn right and in about 50 paces go left through an arch (between houses) joining an enclosed path. Pass an orchard on your left and go up and down a small flight of steps over a bank. Continue and cross over a footbridge and a metal stile. Continue with the stream now on your left to a path junction. Hook left and continue, passing an oast house on your right. At the farm drive go straight across and

continue along the footpath between buildings. Cross a footbridge and join the stream again on its winding course. Cross another footbridge into a large hop field and go straight on along the right side. In about 100 metres, turn right over a stile by a barn, cross a footbridge and then another. Continue with a field on your right and a house on your left. Go straight across a drive and continue, soon joining a high wooden fence on your left. Cross a stile and go directly ahead across the field eventually joining the right hedge. Follow it round to the right and come to the field corner. Turn left over a stile and go along an enclosed footpath, in front of the field hedge. Continue through a gate and cross the next field, keeping directly ahead as the right hedge curves away. Continue to Alders Road. The Dovecote Inn is on the right.

Cross the road and go over a stile opposite. Follow the right side of the field alongside a bungalow and at the end, turn left continuing round the edge of the same field, heading towards a wood. Continue straight on through the wood and when an apple orchard appears in front of you, bear right towards a gate to enter the orchard. Follow way-marked posts uphill, aiming for a gate in the far right corner. Go through and continue under electric cables, then turn right through a gate into Amhurst Bank Road.

The Amhurst Family of Bayhall were large landowners in the 17th century. At Amhurst Hill Farm you can still see hoppers' huts and cookhouses.

Turn left along the road, pass Amhurst Hill Farm and then go on downhill to a bridge at the bottom of the hill. Turn right through woodland.

You can go to Pembury Old Church by looking out for a way-marked post at a gate in the left fence shortly after the beginning of the wood. This gate will lead you through fields passing Kent College on your right to emerge near the church (consult OS map). About 20 minutes there and back.

Continue through the wood keeping close to the left fence. Pass an adventure playground on your left and then turn right in front of a gate. Keep to the main track which winds downhill through the wood with steps on a steep downhill section. Cross a plank footbridge and then go uphill eventually following a fence on your left. Continue along the path high on the left bank of a stream.

Steep sided valleys such as this are typical of the sandstones of the southern half of the lowy of Tonbridge. They account for the abundance of woodland and in consequence, bluebells, wild garlic and occasionally orchids. In mediaeval times, the woods were a rich source of timber, charcoal and grazing for pigs and other livestock.

Arrive at a fence, cross a stile and bear left into a field, then go ahead alongside trees on your right. Look out for a stile in the right fence (shortly before the end of the field) and cross into another field. Keep along the left side of the field, passing a pond on your left and then turn left through a gate into a cherry orchard. Continue alongside the left fence and go over a

stile into an apple orchard. Continue to the end of the left fence by a pylon and bear right in front of a way-marked post along a wide grassy path and then bear left, aiming towards a tall hedge of silver birch trees. Keep the hedge on your right and continue down the right side of the orchard.

Go through a gate in the corner of the orchard to a field and continue for about 100 metres following the right hedge to a corner. Turn right and pass a fishing lake on your left and enter another orchard. Go slightly right along a grass path between trees then bear left to buildings and pass through to a drive emerging on Amhurst Bank Road. Turn left and continue down and up the road passing a byway on your right and shortly (as the road bears left) keep straight ahead through an open gate following a tarmac drive.

 Capel Church will come into view and in the distance, Hadlow Tower. Continue down the hill passing old hoppers' huts in the fields. Arrive at Alders Road, cross over to Church Lane and continue up the lane towards the main entrance of the church.

The church has well preserved 13th century wall paintings (contemporary with the perambulation) and an ancient yew. To visit the church you need to arrive before 4pm.

Continue along Church Lane passing Tanners Farm on your right and in about 100 metres turn right along a public footpath and follow a track into a field. Bear left, go through an open gate and keep ahead then bear right aiming in the direction of a way-marked post in the hedge far to the right. On the way you will pass under electric cables. At the hedge, go through the gate into the lane (Sychem Lane).

Sychem Lane was named after a farm which used to be on the site of the houses; on old maps the farm is named 'Sickhams Farm.'

Turn left and as the road bears left, turn right along a tarmac drive to Lydd Farm. At the end of the straight section of drive, before you reach the clock house, turn left and cross a stile into a field. Continue straight ahead across the field and at the end (the field is very long and thin) turn right over a stile and follow an enclosed path to a junction you may recognise from the outward journey. Keep ahead following the fence on your left with the Alder Stream on your right. Go over the metal stile and footbridge then up and over the steps on the small embankment and along to Five Oak Green.

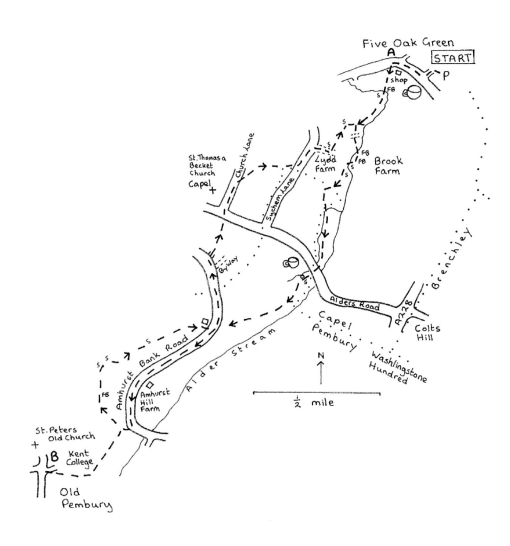

114

6 Old Pembury and Romford

Maps:	OS Explorer 136
Distance:	5.5 miles
Stiles:	5 stiles
Start:	Pembury Old Church; TQ 626428
Transport:	Bus 208; Tonbridge/Pembury Green
Parking:	Old Church (limited)
Refresh:	Pubs and shops; Pembury High St.
	Farm Shops; Downingbury, Pippins

An interesting and pretty woodland walk beginning in the still wooded 'South Frith' forest of Tonbridge and including the fine buildings of Pembury, the woodland site of JMW Turner's painting of Pembury Mill, and views across apple orchards.

'to Dodingebery ...and so as far as the pale of the forest..and so by the pale so the land which is the fee of the earl is within..'

The forest pale of the 'South Frith' and the old Tonbridge Parish boundary is conveniently followed by a public footpath just inside its curved course. You will pass the site of a forest gate, now a major road junction.

The lovely golden sandstone church of Old Pembury, although not open is worth a look. Thought to have existed by the 12th century, it was enlarged by John Culpepper of Bayhall in the 14th century.

Start

Start at St. Peter's Old Church and walk down Old Church Road passing Kent College and then Pembury Waterworks on your left. Continue up towards the A228 Maidstone Road joining the pavement on the left after Redwings Lane. At the junction with Maidstone Road follow the pavement round to the left and spiral uphill crossing the footbridge over the road. Go forward for a short distance and turn right on a footpath which runs alongside the road. Turn left in front of a gate along a path enclosed with high wire fences. This is the line of the old forest pale.

This course of the forest fence hardly changes direction except near the beginning where there is a dog leg turn as the path crosses the boundary bank The woodland here is called 'Forest Wood' (the wood of Tonbridge Forest).

Look for the boundary bank on your left as you continue along, passing pine plantations, coppiced chestnut and silver birch. Eventually pass school grounds and a small graveyard on your left. As the houses come nearer, bear right across a wooden plank footbridge and continue along (ignoring a path on the right) to a major path junction.

Keep straight ahead and go uphill passing houses on your left and woods on your right. Pass an incoming path from the right. Continue ahead and go round a gate, eventually emerging at the junction of Maidstone Road and the old Tonbridge/Hastings Road.

This junction is called Woodsgate, once providing gated entry to the 'South Frith.' The gate was probably across the end of Pembury High Street, a much narrower road then. From Woodsgate, the forest pale continued in the direction of Tunbridge Wells, although the precise course is uncertain.

Turn next left round the petrol station and continue along Pembury High Street to Pembury Green and the Camden Arms.

Pembury High Street was the Hastings/London Road before the A21 by-pass and was once busy with horses and carriages. As a result there are some handsome houses with their stables or 'mews.'

Across the road from the 'Camden Arms' a horse trough commemorates Marjorie Polley, who in 1555 was burnt at the stake in Tonbridge for her Protestant faith.

Pass the Camden Arms and continue along the High Street (now Hastings Road). Pass the war memorial, 'Postillions' and St. Peters Upper Church on your right.

St. Peters Upper Church is open to the public. Consecrated in 1847 it had a completely new interior in 1991. The church once had a 92 foot spire which became dangerous and was removed in 1984.

117

Across the road there are some almshouses built by the Amshurst family of Bayhall in the 18th Century.

Pass the 'King William IV' pub on the left and soon after this turn left down Canterbury Road. At the T junction turn right into Henwood Green Road, passing allotments on your left. Shortly turn left down Woodside Road and then right up Henwood Mount. Continue along a track at the end of the road towards Woodside playing fields. Come to a metal gate and go round it into the sports ground. Keep straight ahead along the right hedge and at the corner go over two stiles.

This is a high point in Pembury and nearby on the right at the Hastings Road the area is called 'Bo Peep.' 'Peep' meaning 'watch' could be the source of the old name Peppingeberia.

After the second stile continue ahead into a field and shortly turn left following a path (Tunbridge Wells Circular Walk, TWCW) alongside a scrubby wood to the field corner. Bear left through holly scrub to a stile in the corner. Cross the stile and continue along the TWCW and High Weald Walk, descending on a grassy path between fields towards a stile at a hedge corner. Go over the stile and along an enclosed path with a garden on your right. Cross a stile to Romford Road. On the right is Kings Toll.

There is a cluster of 'Kings' place names here, suggesting royal ownership of the land probably as part of the manor of Aylesford; an ancient royal estate. This area is close to Sussex and the Kings of Kent appeared to hang on to their lands close to the county boundary.

Turn left along Romford Road with houses on your left and orchard on your right. Go uphill and at the crest, turn right along a track just before a 'Woodlands' sign.

Continue past bungalows and about 100 metres after the last one, turn left through a gate signed Snipe Wood Farm (opposite a way-marked post) and continue along an enclosed track to a T junction with a gate ahead. Turn right and go along an enclosed path to open woodland. Soon come to a footpath junction with a way-marked post. Continue ahead still following the TWCW and High Weald Walk (HWW). Continue through coppice woods and go downhill along a track to a four way sign post where the track bends sharply right. Follow the High Weald Walk straight ahead and proceed along a footpath through woods to a brick footbridge.

 *This brick structure is thought to be the site of a dam between two millponds*

where JMW Turner painted his watercolour of Pembury Mill (called Herrings Mill on old OS maps). The watercolour shows hills in the background which would be visible without the trees. There are other possible sites and the debate about the exact location continues.

Continue uphill between overgrown orchards and arrive at a T junction. Turn left and go alongside a hedge on your right, towards a wooden shelter. At the grassy area in front of the shelter turn sharply right through a field corner into an orchard (Pippins Farm). Go along the left side of the orchard passing a house on your left and come to a pond. Turn left around the pond and go across to a yard between farm buildings. Continue ahead on a long farm drive to the old Maidstone Road, passing Pippins Farm Shop on your left.

Pippins Farm is a large apple business. This is good orchard land compared with the woodland passed through earlier. It is gentler, of open aspect, and not so damp.

Continue to the old Maidstone Road, cross over and go straight along the opposite drive round to the entrance of Downingbury Farm Shop.

Downingbury (Dodingbury of the perambulation) is just outside the lowy and the forest pale of the South Frith. On this last part of the walk you will approach the line of the forest pale again along Old Church Road.

Walk past the entrance to the farm shop and on round the building, passing right of a pylon, to a bridge over the Maidstone Road. Turn right across the bridge, then go left down steps and continue on a grassy track between a tall hedge on the left and field on your right. Take the first right downhill towards the reservoir, bear left before an orchard and continue to a grassy area. Go across and emerge on a lane (Redwings Lane). Turn left, arrive at a T junction and then turn right along Old Church Road back to the start.

The South Frith forest pale runs parallel with Old Church Road, a little way to your left.

© Crown copyright 2013 Ordnance Survey 100054134

121

Pembury Green and the Pantiles

Maps:	OS Explorer 136
Distance:	7.5 miles, (3.5 to 4, one way)
Stiles:	2 stiles (can be avoided)
Start:	Pembury Green; TQ 625407
Transport:	Bus 208; Tonbridge/Pembury Gr;
	6/6A; Tunbridge Wells/Pembury Gr.
Parking:	Pembury Green
Refresh:	Pubs,cafes and shops,
	Pembury and Tunbridge Wells

This is a walk of contrasts, starting in the country with glorious views and ending in Tunbridge Wells High Street with its buzzing cafes, pubs and shops. The approximate course of the South Frith forest pale can be seen most of the way and in Tunbridge Wells, the most southerly point of the perambulation is reached. The walk can be achieved without stiles and there is a good bus service between Pembury and Tunbridge Wells for a shorter one way walk.

'and so by the pale to Bromelegeregg which is all within..and Sunningelegh and Hocubery of the service of the King be without..and so to the oak called Wogebohe..'

'Bromelegeregg,' meaning 'broom ridge' is probably the ridge on which runs the A264 Pembury Road. This road continues to Crescent Road in Tunbridge Wells where in the 16th century there was a small hamlet with a similar name, Bromelerge. Sunningelegh (Sunninglye) is the name of a farm near Frant and Hocubery is modern Hawkenbury which is passed on this walk. In Tunbridge Wells the perambulation reaches the most southerly point. The oak tree of 'wogeboh' possibly became the meeting point of parish and county boundaries at the church of King Charles the Martyr.

Start at Pembury Green, pass the Camden Arms on your right and turn right down Chalket Lane. Go through a pair of open white gates and come to a white gate on your left (to avoid the two stiles and livestock on this walk continue down Chalket Lane to a path junction at the bottom, then pick up the directions at ** next page). Turn left in front of the gate of Great Bayhall House and continue on an enclosed path. Keep ahead in the same direction and eventually you will come alongside the A21 in a deep cutting on your right. Continue to the footbridge and cross over the A21. Go straight on through a wood, following a high wooden fence on your left. Follow the fence round to the right, ignoring a path going left and continue ahead to a path junction with good views from the field gate.

The ridge over to the right could be 'Bromelegeregg' and the approximate course of the South Frith forest pale. The farm on the hill in front of you is Little Bayhall Farm which you will walk through.

Turn right at the junction in the direction of the Tunbridge Wells Circular Walk (TWCW). Continue along a wide track and after about 100 metres turn left over a stile into a field. Continue downhill, straight across the field taking a course in the direction of the high farm on the opposite hill. Go towards a tall, dense clump of trees at the bottom. At the field edge, cross a stile and a footbridge then turn right along a track (Chalket Lane). Take the next left along a track, following the TWCW.

** (If you came all the way down Chalket Lane, turn right at the bottom along a track following the 'Tunbridge Wells Circular Walk').

Continue through woodland and then go uphill on the right side of a field. Go through a gateway onto a paved lane (High Woods Lane). Pass cottages on your right and continue along the lane through Little Bayhall Farm.

The river in the valley on your left is the Teise which is followed by the Kent/Sussex County boundary. In the valley, there was a grand country house called Bayhall with formal gardens, demolished in 1960. A large oil painting of it hangs in Tunbridge Wells Museum. The site was once a mediaeval moat and the home of the Culpeppers who may have taken their name from an old form of Pembury (Peppingeberia, 12th century). They moved away and were followed by the Amhurst and Camden families whose names remain in buildings, roads and pubs nearby.

Continue through woods and on along the lane until you pass the Royals Indoor Bowls Club on your right. Go round the gate and continue along High Woods Lane passing 'Marl Pits allotments' on your right.

Marl Pits are a common feature in the landscape. By the 13th century and before artificial fertilisers, marl was often dug out of pits to spread on fields. Believed to be lime rich, it was used in areas far from chalk. Many of them are now ponds.

Continue to a T junction (Halls Hole Road), turn left and soon reach the busy Forest Road. Keep left and continue round Forest Road, passing a shop and a church on your left. Continue to the island crossing, cross over, turn right and then left along the 'no through road,' (Camden Park).

This is Hawkenbury ('Hocubury'), recorded on the perambulation as belonging to the King and just outside the lowy of Tonbridge.

The road becomes a path and takes you through light woodland with fields appearing on your right. Emerge onto a road, turn right and after a few paces turn left along a Restricted Byway just after houses called Hollyshaw Close. Come out at Claremont School and go past the

entrance, then keep ahead along a path to the right of Glen Cottage. Arrive at a T junction with Claremont Road, cross over and turn left.

Claremont Road is not an old name but it is very appropriate on this hill belonging once to the Clares of Tonbridge Castle.

Pass Norfolk, Grecian and Buckingham Roads on your right and then turn right into Grove Park. Continue down the left side of the park.

Grove Park was a gift from the Villiers family in 1703 to the Wells. They lived at Somerhill and were owners of South Frith Manor, created out of the old hunting forest which extended from Tonbridge to Tunbridge Wells.

Keep ahead and leave the park down a narrow cobbled street (South Grove). Emerge onto the High Street and turn left continuing along a raised pavement. At the end, go straight on along a pedestrian street towards the church of King Charles the Martyr. Turn right in front of the church and continue past the entrance to the other side (south wall).

Open to the public, 11am to 3pm each day, this delightful church is worth a visit for the handsome baroque ceilings among many other things.

In the brickwork below the second window you can see the Tonbridge/Speldhurst Parish boundary (also marked on the opposite wall and on the interior walls).

Away from the church wall, a boundary stone is set in the pavement, marking the county and parish boundaries. Perhaps the oak tree of 'Wogebohe' was here at the southern end of the lowy.

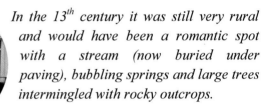

In the 13th century it was still very rural and would have been a romantic spot with a stream (now buried under paving), bubbling springs and large trees intermingled with rocky outcrops.

Across Neville Road and just within the Pantiles is the Chalybeate (iron rich) spring which Lord North discovered in 1606 had healing qualities, and so began the life of Tunbridge Wells.

Continue alongside the south wall of the church and go straight ahead along a brick paved path called Cumberland Walk.

Cumberland Walk is named after Richard Cumberland, the late 18th century Playwright who lived locally. There are some remarkable houses including one made of flint pebbles. Cumberland Walk follows the approximate line of the old Kent/Sussex boundary.

Arrive at a road, turn right and then shortly left along Upper Cumberland Walk which becomes a road with houses on both sides. Pass the Tunbridge Wells Lawn Tennis Club on your right, and then go straight on along a narrow path, following the Tunbridge Wells to Hastings railway line on your left. Cross over via a footbridge.

Arrive at a road (Cavendish Drive), turn right, pass Delves Avenue and continue to a mini roundabout. Turn right along Farncombe Road and pass another mini roundabout to the junction with Forest Road. Turn left into Forest Road and after the 'Spread Eagle' pub, turn right along Boundary Road. Come to a T junction and turn right along Hawkenbury Road, passing Hawkenbury Mead on your left and then Maryland Road on your right. Pass hockey pitches on your left and continue along the road.

Turn left after a car park at a footpath sign 'High Weald Walk.' Go alongside a holly hedge on your left and come to a metal hurdle. After the hurdle, ignore the first left and in a few paces fork left. Continue to a path junction and go straight on along the High Weald Walk. Soon cross a track and continue ahead. Arrive eventually at High Woods Lane.

Turn right and continue along the lane to the end, passing the cottages on your left. Keep right going into the field and go downhill along the left side. Keep ahead through woodland and reach a T junction. Turn left along Chalket Lane and go uphill passing between the gates of Chalket and Howfield Farms. Continue over the A21 road bridge and go straight on along Chalket Lane to Pembury Green.

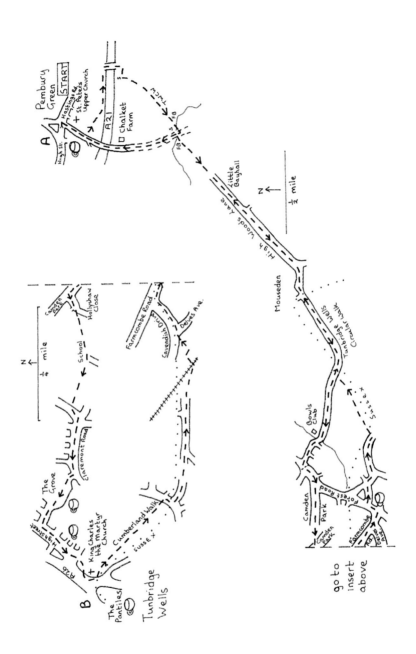

128

8 Tunbridge Wells and Rusthall

Maps:	OS Explorer 147
Distance:	6 miles
Stiles:	3 stiles
Start:	Neville Street; TQ 582388
Transport:	Trains; Tonbridge/Tunbridge Wells
	Bus; 7, 77 Tonbridge/Tunbridge Wells
Parking:	Tunbridge Wells
Refresh:	Pubs,cafes and shops,
	Tunbridge Wells & Rusthall

This walk is hilly and romantic with long woodland walks, rocky outcrops, streams and lush pastures. Speldhurst and Rusthall are on or close to the route. End on the romantic theme with sunset on Tunbridge Wells Common.

'and so to the domus of Willelmi de Colverdene which is within.. and so through the middle of the wood of Hertesell so all the tenants of Wechelstone are without..'

The perambulation is followed almost exactly. Hugging the old Tonbridge/Speldhurst Parish boundary it leaves the South Frith pale and skirts round the 'South Borough.' The land of William of Colverden, is still present in the numerous 'Culverden' street names.

129

The route passes Speldhurst, an important centre of Washlingstone hundred which perhaps precluded it from the lowy of Tonbridge.

Start at the boundary stone set in paving outside the church of King Charles the Martyr and cross Neville Street towards the Pantiles. Turn right and cross London Road to the 'The Forum,' (*built as public 'rest rooms' in 1939 and now a popular music venue*). Walk up the right side of 'The
Forum' and at a path junction turn right and continue straight on, until you emerge again on London Road. Cross over at the island, turn left and then bear right along red brick paving, following the Inner London Road.

The Inner London Road was the west boundary of the great South Frith. This large forest in due course became part of the estate of Somerhill and the houses and roads bear the names of Somerhill and its former owners.

Tunbridge Wells is built on sandstone and between here and Speldhurst there are massive walls made of it and solitary outcrops.

Continue straight on passing Church Road, York Road, Dudley Road and Lime Hill Road. Cross Mount Ephraim Road and then cross over Mount Ephraim at the pelican crossing. Turn left going back along Mount Ephraim and then turn right down Royal Chase.

The perambulation continued along Royal Chase. To the right is Culverden belonging in the 13th century to William of Colverden. It was part of the 'South Borough' of the lowy of Tonbridge.

130

Continue straight on at the cross roads down Byng Road. At the T junction, turn right along Culverden Down, go down and then up and just before Coniston Avenue on your left, switchback left down a footpath to a stream and continue with the stream on your left and gardens on your right. Continue to a road (Coniston Avenue) and go forward to an unmade road and a high wire fence. Continue with the fence on your left passing a waterworks. Fork right along the wider track and continue to a kissing gate.

This is Hurst Wood, possibly derived from Speldhurst. It is wholly within the parish and as you leave the wood you will rejoin the perambulation route along the Tonbridge lowy boundary.

Go through the kissing gate and fork right uphill, continuing along the widest track. Keep ahead for some distance and look out for an old iron gatepost half buried in a beech tree on your right. Continue and eventually cross a stile by a metal gate and go along an enclosed path. At a path junction bear left downhill, cross over a stream and continue up the narrow path to Broomhill Road. Turn right and Salomons Tower comes into view.

Salomons is now a campus of Christ Church University, Canterbury but in 1855 it was the home of David Salomons, Lord Mayor of London and one of the founders of the predecessor of the Nat West Bank. His nephew David Lionel was a scientist and he carried out many electrical experiments at the estate after he inherited it in 1873. He installed one of the first domestic electric lighting systems, powered by a coal fired generator. There is a museum in the estate detailing his many inventions (admission free).

131

You are again following the perambulation route with Tonbridge on your right, Washlingstone hundred and Speldhurst on your left.

Continue down Broomhill Road, pass the entrance to Mill Farm and then turn left just in front of a high stone wall. Continue alongside a stream on this enclosed path, eventually leaving the stream and ascending the hill with glimpses of Speldhurst over on the left.

The name Speldhurst is first recorded in the 8th century as belonging to the Bishop of Rochester. It was a centre of Washlingstone hundred which is probably why it remained outside the lowy, despite the nearness of the land hungry and powerful Norman Clares.

At the top of the hill arrive at a road (Speldhurst Road), cross over and continue ahead up stone steps and through a kissing gate to join a narrow enclosed footpath. Continue to a kissing gate, go through to a T junction and turn left on the Tunbridge Wells Circular Walk (TWCW). At the next kissing gate, go through to a field and turn right leaving the TWCW and joining the Wealdway (WW). Cross two fields and two stiles along the right hedge and continue to a road (Stockland Green Road).

Turn left and continue down Stockland Green Road to Forge House. Turn right through a tall metal gate and cross the drive. Go downhill on a footpath which becomes steep with steps. Cross a stile and a stream into the yard of an animal food store (once Speldhurst Mill). Go straight on through the yard (the mill still has remnants of a wheel), continue uphill along the drive to a road (Speldhurst Hill) and cross over.

You can go up the hill to see the church (with Pre-Raphaelite stained glass) and visit the pub and shop or go downhill continuing the walk.

132

Turn left down the hill and next right along Lower Green Road. In about 100 metres (as the road bears left) turn right along a footpath into Shadwell Wood. Continue straight ahead for some distance (½ mile) along an obvious track. At a point where a major path joins from the right, (the slope on the right falls away steeply here) go forward downhill for about 20 metres and then turn left up a bank, where a way-marked post is pointing you in the direction of the 'Tunbridge Wells Circular Walk Link Route.'

Soon go over a stile into a field. Go directly across and over a stile in the field corner and then continue along an enclosed path joining eventually a wide track. Pass allotments, timber yards etc. and emerge in Rusthall on Lower Green Road. Turn right, then  cross over to the 'Red Lion' and continue along Lower Green Road until you pass the 'White Hart' on your left. Fork left along the pavement across the Green to the junction with Rusthall Road.

Cross over and bear left along a footpath crossing the Common. Continue ahead, merging eventually with Langton Road. Continue past the Tunbridge Wells Golf Club and Spa Hotel on your left and come to a drinking fountain memorial. At the memorial, cross over Langton Road towards the former Major York Pub and continue down the left side of the building on a paved footpath. Pass a row of houses on your right and cross the entrance to Neville Park. Continue until you cross over a road called Hungershall Park and then bear left across Tunbridge Wells Common.

Eventually you will pass a car park on your right and emerge on a road (Major Yorks Road). Cross over and go right for a few paces, then bear left towards a white building. Pass the building on your right and continue to the London Road (A26). Cross over a Zebra Crossing and turn left towards the church of King Charles the Martyr. Any of the passages on the right will lead you to the Pantiles where you can view the site of the chalybeate spring that began the story of Tunbridge Wells' phenomenal growth from the late 17th century.

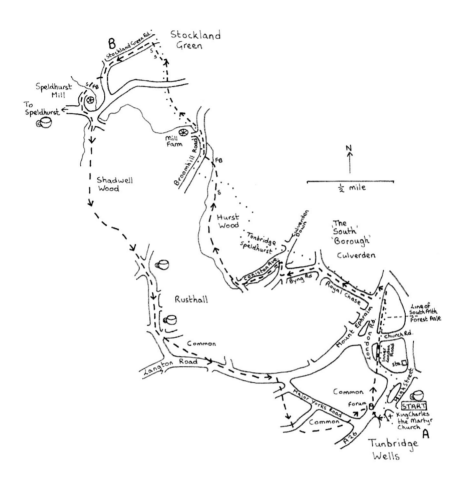

© Crown copyright 2013 Ordnance Survey 100054134

9 Speldhurst and Poundsbridge

Maps:	OS Explorer 147
Distance:	4.5 miles
Stiles:	16 stiles
Start:	The George and Dragon; TQ 554414
Transport:	Bus 282 Tunbridge Wells/Speldhurst
Parking:	Speldhurst Village
Refresh:	The George and Dragon and shop, Speldhurst

This is a challenging walk with steep gradients and many stiles. The reward is a picture postcard panorama for virtually the entire walk. In between there are some fascinating old houses and farms including the dramatic and historic village of Speldhurst. The church has beautiful pre-Raphaelite stained glass.

'and so through the middle of the wood of Hertesell so all the tenants of Wechelstone are without..and directly to the messuage of William Shrufin..and so to Wolstonesland and Horgate and Hegedonne....'

The perambulation followed the valley of Bentham Brook, where some of the listed names can be found. Washlingstone hundred is believed to be centred on Speldhurst, where Saxons met at the original 'wechel stone' (now lost). This might explain why Speldhurst and district remained 'without.'

136

Start

Start at the George and Dragon Inn and set off down Speldhurst Hill passing a road junction and 'Wallers' on your right. Continue to the entrance of an animal food store at the bottom of the hill on your left. Cross over the road and go along the drive to the store (following the Weald Way). Go down through the yard passing old Speldhurst Mill on your right. Cross over a stream and go over a stile. Continue steeply uphill and then along an enclosed path to emerge at the high metal gate of Forge House. Go through the gate into Stockland Green Road. Turn left and go uphill to Stockland Green until you reach the junction with Franks Hollow Road.

Turn left down Franks Hollow Road with good views across to Bidborough Ridge. Pass the entrance to Scriventon House on your left. The road will steepen and when it turns right, go left at a footpath sign and over a stile. Cross the field with views across Bentham Brook Valley to Bidborough Ridge. At the far left corner of the field, go over a stile and continue along the left side of the next field. At the next corner, cross a stile, bear right across a yard and go over a stone/brick stile.

You are passing through Scriventon Farm, 'the messuage of William Shrufin' (sc is pronounced sh in Old English). The boundary of the lowy followed the brook, so William's house was 'without' while Bidborough Ridge on the other side was 'within.'

Pass a barn on your right and continue downhill along a paved track, looking ahead to the Medway Valley and Speldhurst Hill on the left. As you approach the valley bottom cross a footbridge and bear right. Follow a stream on your right, which is joined by a second stream, Bentham Brook.

137

The lowy boundary followed Bentham Brook and from here you pass into Tonbridge. The wood over to the right is called Little Tonbridge Wood. The jurors would have come this way from Scriventon.

Bear left along the track and cross a stile to a residential road. Continue between houses to Barden Road; turn left and shortly right along a drive towards Barden Furnace Farm and Old Barn. As the drive bears right, continue ahead along an enclosed track to a stile. Go over and continue ahead along the left side of the field, passing ponds on your left. Over to the right you can see the buildings of Barden Furnace Farm and Mill.

This once part of Tonbridge (now in Bidborough) is centred on Barden Mill. It was connected with Barden Park and both areas are thought to have once belonged to Eynsford Manor but became part of the lowy of Tonbridge with the arrival of the Normans

There was a mill here in 1086 and an ironworks could have been here in mediaeval times. Iron, timber and plentiful, fast flowing water were available to encourage a local iron industry. It supplied arms for the Parliamentary Army in the English Civil War.

Along the route there are a number of ponds on the left side of the path. It is possible that they were all connected to the mill as holding ponds for water. At times when the water level in the stream was low the ponds could be emptied in sequence to allow the mill wheel to continue turning.

Stone Wood on the left could be a shortened form of 'Wolstonesland.'

Continue along the left side of fields and eventually go over a stile at a pond. Continue on the right side of the pond and go over another stile. Keep ahead passing between two telegraph poles and join a field hedge on your left. Continue to the next corner and go over the stile. Pass another pond on your left and continue along the left side of the field.

Over to the right there is a very distinct conical hill; called High Dens on tithe maps, it will be the 'Hegedonne' of the perambulation (within the lowy).

At the corner, go over the stile and go down steps to Penshurst Road at Poundsbridge. Turn right to the junction and then left past an interesting Elizabethan house.

The house at Poundsbridge has a date of 1593 and the initials WD (William Durkinghole). Durkinghole is a family name long associated with the local area and in the perambulation it is mentioned twice associated with property in the area of Penshurst and Chiddingstone Causeway.

After the house turn right along Coopers Lane and continue to Hamsell Farm. Pass 'Little Colnbrook' on your left and shortly after the houses, turn left on a public footpath. Bear right uphill, through three fields. The gaps in the hedges are signed but as a simple guide; the first is in the right hedge (towards the top), the second in the top hedge/fence at the centre and the third in the top right corner.

You will be rewarded with one of the best views in the weald.

Go through a gate back into Coopers Lane and turn left. Continue uphill to the junction with Poundsbridge Lane and go directly opposite to a stile, now joining the Weald Way (WW). Go along an enclosed path through woods and  ponds and cross a stile on the left. Cross a field and go over another stile. Continue across another field towards the left corner and woodland. Go over another stile, turn left and proceed downhill (ignoring paths to the left and right), along a woodland path. Descend steeply to a stream and cross via a footbridge, then go uphill on the other side. At the top go left in front of a house and garage (WW) and emerge on Bullingstone Lane.

Turn right and pass Bullingstone Farm and the Old Farmhouse on your left, then turn left at a footpath sign. Continue along an enclosed path, cross a stile, pass between fields and go over another stile. Pass between gardens and houses, maintaining direction, and eventually go through a kissing gate to Penshurst Road at Speldhurst. Turn right and follow the road round, passing the church on your left to the 'George and Dragon' Inn.

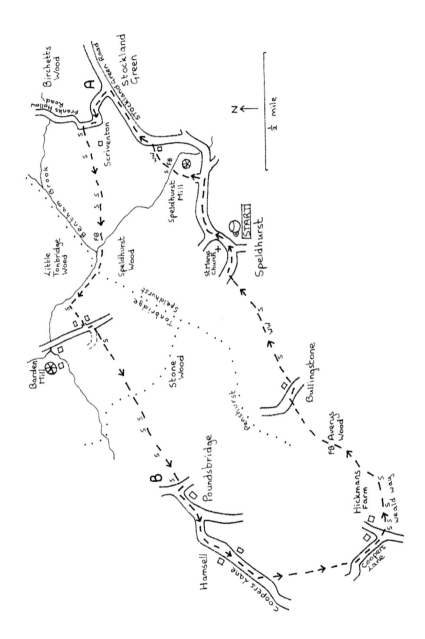

141

Penshurst and the Medway Valley

Maps:	OS Explorer 147
Distance:	3.5 miles
Stiles:	5 stiles
Start:	Entrance Penshurst Place; TQ 527437
Parking:	Penshurst Place and village
Refresh:	Cafes and shop, Penshurst

This very gentle walk is entirely in the wide Medway valley with glorious views across the ring of surrounding hills. Pillboxes,

footbridges, meadows, arable fields and sky are the main features but interesting old farms and houses are dotted about and the walk passes through the picturesque village of Penshurst. Penshurst Place has a magnificent 14th century hall and beautiful gardens.

'..and so to Horgate and Hegedonne..to a sort of hill called Smethedonne..and so to the garden of Penecestr..'

It is possible to identify some of the places described, as there are precise topographic details such as the middle of a wood or a hill. This walk follows very nearly the line of the perambulation route. Penshurst was the home of Sir Stephen; his house has disappeared but his garden and estate remain.

Stephen's effigy is in the Sidney Chapel in Penshurst Church. Penshurst Place has been the home of the Sidney family for more than 450 years. If you look at your OS map you will see the logo contains an arrowhead (pheon); a heraldic symbol of the Sidney family. It is thought that Henry
Sidney introduced it as a mark of government property (most often seen on cartoons of prison uniform) in the 17th century when he was Master General of the Ordnance.

Start

Start outside the entrance arch of Penshurst Place and walk towards the village, passing the road junction. Continue along the High Street (becomes Fordcombe Road) passing the shop, the village school and houses (take care as there is no pavement here). Finally pass 'The Glebe' and come to the bridge over the Eden (Long Bridge).

Immediately after the bridge, turn left down steps along a footpath. Cross a footbridge and continue directly across a field up towards a house (Ford Place). Cross a track and go through a small stand of conifer trees to a drive. Cross over and continue downhill along an enclosed track passing a wood on your left. Cross over a ditch and keep directly ahead across an arable field marked out with wooden posts, aiming for two large oak trees.

Pass between the trees and right of a hidden pill box and then pass a footbridge (over the Medway) on your left. Shortly bear right across the field to another pill box and continue towards a patch of scrub in the field corner. Come to the river bank, go through a hedge and turn left to follow the river until you reach the next field corner. Turn right, away from the river and continue on the left side of the field to the next corner.

143

Go left over a stile by a metal gate, bear slightly right over the brow of the hill and then go down towards a metal footbridge over the Medway, which you cross. Continue straight across the field, soon going alongside a ditch on your left and go through a gateway. Bear right across the next field aiming towards a chapel and church yard ahead. Follow a footpath to the left of the church yard and emerge on a lane (Coopers Lane). Turn left and continue to the junction with Poundsbridge Hill. Turn left down the road passing an Elizabethan house on your right to the junction at Poundsbridge.

The house at Poundsbridge has a date of 1593 and the initials WD (William Durkinghole). Durkinghole is a family name long associated with the local area and in the perambulation it is mentioned twice associated with property in the area of Penshurst and Chiddingstone Causeway.

Turn left along Poundsbridge Lane passing a red pillar box on your right and cross a bridge over Bentham Brook. Pass Bowens Cottage on your left and Bowens Farm on your right.

The old parish boundary of Penshurst/Tonbridge crossed this lane just uphill of Bowens Farm, so the farm could be at the site of Horgate outside the lowy.

On the road at the top of the hill there is an old smithy and probably not the first. The hill was an important source of timber and iron ore and if there was mediaeval iron working at Barden it is also likely that a smith would set up shop here and give the hill its name 'smethedonne'.

Turn left just before the next house on your left and enter a small drive. Go through a field gate ahead and continue along the right hedge until you come to the corner. Go over a stile and continue along an enclosed path, going straight on and then left. Come to a junction and turn right. Follow the enclosed path and continue to Old Swaylands manor house.

Turn left along a track just after the manor house and pass the ivy clad 'Stone Cottage' on your right. Continue ahead along an enclosed path following a high brick wall on your right. Come to a gate and go through continuing along the right side of a field alongside the grounds of Swaylands on your right.

Swaylands is recorded in the 13th century. The lowy boundary and the jurors passed through obliquely up this hill of 'Smethedonne', as the old Tonbridge/Penshurst parish boundary did.

The fields to the left were once hop gardens and you can still see occasional hop poles in the hedges.

At a metal gate, go through and continue along the field edge. A fence will eventually appear on your left as the track bears right. Penshurst Village is now visible across the Medway. The river has turned a corner and the valley is narrow enough here to make a good crossing point. Continue through a metal gate and arrive at Rogues Hill. Turn left to Penshurst. Cross over two bridges and arrive at the entrance to Penshurst Place.

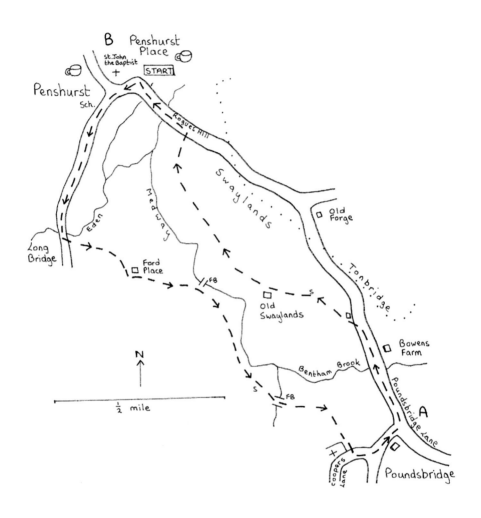

146

11 # Penshurst and the Eden Valley

Maps:	OS Explorer 147
Distance:	5.5 miles
Stiles:	8 stiles
Start:	Entrance, Penshurst Place; TQ 527437
Transport:	Trains; Penshurst/Tonbridge
	Penshurst Station is in Chiddingstone Causeway
Parking:	Penshurst Place and Village
Refresh:	Cafes and shop, Penshurst
	The Little Brown Jug, Chiddingstone Causeway

Pass through green pastures, parkland, exotic woods and enjoy distant views as you circle round the Eden Valley. Penshurst Place with its magnificent 14th century hall and gardens, the church and village are all worth exploring. There is a stretch of quite busy road.

'to the garden of Penecestr and directly to Redelef..and from Redelef to Durkynghale ..which is the fee of the Earl..'

Penshurst and Redleaf are still places today, but Durkynghale is hard to trace. In old deeds the name is associated with the Eden Valley at Chiddingstone where parish boundaries met and land disputes were likely. The perambulation follows the Leigh Parish boundary.

Start outside the entrance arch to Penshurst Place facing the village. Turn right up steps to pass through the picturesque buildings of 'Leicester Square' and continue to the entrance of the Church.

Leicester Square is a pleasing mix of old 16th century and newer 1850 buildings (by George Devey, architect).

The Church is open during the day and inside the Sidney Chapel there is an effigy of Sir Stephen of Penshurst lying on the floor. He is in chain mail with his hand on the hilt of his sword as if to draw. As Constable of Dover Castle and Warden of the Cinque Ports and an itinerant justice in the King's service, he presided over the perambulation in Tonbridge. He must have had a grand house in Penshurst although it has since been buried beneath still grander houses.

Continue past the church and go through a kissing gate into Penshurst Park. Follow the wooden fence on your right and where the path forks, keep ahead. Again where there is another fork, keep ahead passing left of a group of conifer trees. Come to a kissing gate, cross the drive and go through another kissing gate opposite. Continue ahead through an avenue of trees passing a cricket ground on your right. At the end of the cricket ground follow the track as it bears right between two trees. Continue heading slightly left so that you will go alongside the avenue of trees on your left. Pass large oaks on your right and continue to a kissing gate ahead. Go through and continue ahead and uphill aiming at a house on the hilltop and woodland higher up on the left.

Over to the far right is the ancient Sidney Oak thought to be nearly 500 years old and planted at the birth of Sir Philip Sidney. The Sidney family, now Viscounts de L'Isle (once Earls of Leicester) have owned Penshurst since 1552. It was recently named as one of the 50 greatest British trees.

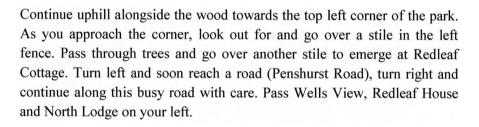

Continue uphill alongside the wood towards the top left corner of the park. As you approach the corner, look out for and go over a stile in the left fence. Pass through trees and go over another stile to emerge at Redleaf Cottage. Turn left and soon reach a road (Penshurst Road), turn right and continue along this busy road with care. Pass Wells View, Redleaf House and North Lodge on your left.

The perambulation and parish boundary goes directly to Redleaf (Redelef), crossing the road from Penshurst Park and continuing between Redleaf House and North Lodge.

Redleaf today is noted for the exotic trees planted in the grounds and neighbouring woods. William Wells (shipbuilder) who resided there in the

early 19th century was the most important patron of the artist, Edwin Landseer (who painted animals including the famous stag, 'Monarch of the Glen'). He had a large collection of Landseer's paintings, now dispersed. His successor (also William Wells) was a champion rifle shot and set up a volunteer rifle range in Penshurst Park which is marked on old O.S. Maps.

Continue along Penshurst Road passing a road junction. About 200 metres after the junction, turn left through a gate into Redleaf Wood. Continue and go straight ahead at a junction with a forest track. Go more or less directly ahead (as much as the winding path allows) and you will descend gradually towards a footbridge at the bottom of the wood. Go over a stile and then the footbridge to emerge at the corner of a field.

You are now in Durkynghale country. There is a 13th century deed in which Stephen of Penshurst allows William de Durkynghale to overwinter his sheep on common land here. Durkynghale is a name found commonly in the area from the 13th century onwards, eventually becoming shortened to Durtnall. In old deeds the name is associated with the river Eden, nearly a mile downstream of here.

Turn left and keep the stream on your left until you reach Moorden Farm buildings. Go past an open barn on your left and then turn left in front of a beech hedge to follow the track to the road. At the road (Station Hill) turn right and just after Moorden Oast, fork left at the road junction and continue to the car park at Penshurst Station.

You are walking through an extended part of Leigh Parish as the boundary swings west (left) to the river Eden. Durkynghale lands were in this area and were disputed lands as they seemed to straddle the Leigh/Penshurst/Chiddingstone boundaries and were intermingled with lands of the Archbishop and the Clares.

At the car park turn left over a stile by a field gate and follow the right hedge. Go through a gateway and continue across the field to the far hedge. Turn left and continue alongside the hedge and a stream. Look for a field entrance in the right hedge and turn right here, cross a footbridge and continue along the left hedge of the next field. Go over a stile in the corner and continue uphill, still following the left side of the field towards the oasts of Beckett's Farm. About half way there, look for a stile in the left hedge and go over it.

Continue along the right side of the field and keep ahead passing through into another field. Continue to the corner and go over a stile. Go directly ahead across another field aiming for the right corner, where there is a (concealed) footbridge. Cross over and go straight across the next field towards a field gate on the far side, at the road. Near the end of the field, come alongside the river Eden on your left. Go through the gate to the road and turn left across Vexour Bridge.

Go straight ahead through the entrance to Vexour. Continue up the drive and near the top where it starts to bear left, turn right through a patch of brushwood and emerge into a field. Turn left and continue along the left side of the field, passing the buildings of Vexour on your left. At the top of the rise, pass a three way post and continue along the left hedge to a large metal barn. Bear right across the field, along a grassy path towards the buildings of Chantlers, then bear left passing a house on your right. After the house, turn right and go along a drive to Weller's Town Road.

Turn left and continue to Weller's Town. Cross over a bridge and go uphill passing rows of cottages. After the last house continue along the road, turning left at the first footpath sign and go over a stile. Cross the field downhill along a broken line of trees, go over a footbridge and through a kissing gate.

Go uphill towards the left end of a range of farm buildings (used to be painted pink with trompe d'oeil windows) and go through a metal gate on the left side of the buildings to a bridleway. The little hamlet here is called Wat Stock. Turn left and continue along the bridleway with good views of the Eden Valley and beyond. As you come closer to the river you will see a farmhouse and oast on the opposite bank.

This is Doubleton, the 13th century dwelling place of another Durkynghale called Dubel. The name had a number of variant spellings but whether 'hale' or 'holes' the name suggests a waterside location such as found here and elsewhere in the Eden valley.

Arrive at a junction (entrance to Salmans Farm on the right) and turn left. Soon cross over the Eden on a bridge with brick parapet. Continue along the road and emerge on Penshurst Road, opposite Penshurst Place. Turn right to the junction and left to the entrance of Penshurst Place.

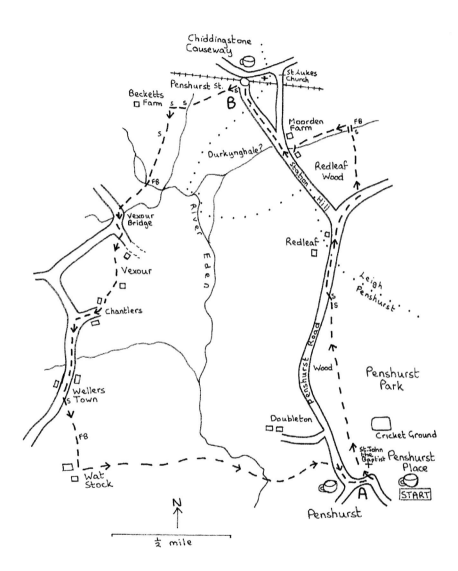

Chiddingstone
Causeway

St Lukes
Church

Penshurst St.

Becketts
Farm

B

Moorden
Farm

FB

Durkynghale?

Redleaf
Wood

River Eden

Vexour
Bridge

Vexour

Redleaf

Leigh
Penshurst

Chantlers

Penshurst Road

Wood

Penshurst
Park

Wellers
Town

FB

Doubleton

Cricket Ground

Wat
Stock

St John
the Baptist

Penshurst
Place

START

A

Penshurst

N

½ mile

© Crown copyright 2013 Ordnance Survey 100054134

Chiddingstone and Coppings

Maps:	OS Explorer 147
Distance:	4.5 miles/2 stiles **or** 5.5 miles/12 stiles
Start:	Penshurst Station; TQ 519465
Transport:	Trains; Penshurst/Tonbridge
	Penshurst Station is in Chiddingstone Causeway
Parking:	Penshurst side of station or Chid. Causeway
Refresh:	The Little Brown Jug, Chiddingstone Causeway
	The Greyhound, Charcott

This landscape of wealden clay is very distinctive as you gently ascend northwards towards the greensand ridge. The heavy clays seem intractable when ploughed but cereals are grown in large rolling fields. In among them, streams weave through small copses and there are wide views throughout. The directions allow for the walk to be shortened.

'through the middle of Rissettes to Coppingsland and so next to the land of the Prior of Tonbridge ..within..'

From the start the Leigh Parish boundary curves north eastwards, nearly to Weald, and footpaths follow it all the way round a large area called Coppings, then Priory Farm and a little further on, Nizels. These place names next door to each other, have survived for over seven centuries.

Start

From the car park at Penshurst Station (on the other side of the track from the Little Brown Jug), go over the footbridge and exit the station. Cross over the road to the Little Brown Jug, turn right and go uphill passing St Lukes Church over on the right. Turn left along a tarmac footpath opposite a road junction and continue to the next road (Camp Hill).

The huge fields on the right were once the site of Penshurst Airfield during the two World Wars. In peacetime it was used for light aircraft and as an emergency landing strip for civil aircraft. The Leigh Parish boundary runs alongside this path and so this is the most likely perambulation route. In 1258 this area was called 'Herrings Heath' and the fields were still called Herringslands on c1840 tithe maps.

At Camp Hill, turn right and first left towards Charcott. Keep ahead, going off the road and along a track signed Charcott Farm, passing Little Keepers on your right. Look out for a gate on your right, go through and bear left across the field, passing buildings on your left. Continue to a kissing gate, go through and keep ahead alongside a hedge on your left. At the hedge corner, descend on a grassy track to Wickhurst Brook.

The long hedge on your left which stays with you for much of this walk is the Leigh Parish boundary.

Cross over the footbridge, go uphill and continue until you rejoin the boundary hedge keeping it on your left. Go through a gap in the field corner and continue ahead alongside the hedge. Where the hedge ends, go straight on towards a wood. Keep on the left side of the wood and eventually cross a footbridge. Turn right then almost immediately left uphill following the fence on your left.

Go through another field, now following a line of trees on your left. Arrive at a clump of trees, concealing a pond. Skirt round the right side of the pond to the field corner. Turn right and as you follow the hedge on your left, look for a gate in the hedge line.

The field on your right is called 'Coppingsfield' on tithe maps and is part of a large estate centred on Coppings Farm.

The Leigh Parish boundary continues along this hedge going towards the Priory Farm lands ahead. The site of Tonbridge Priory is now buried under the railway station and car parks.

Turn left through the gate, go straight across the field to a corner and then follow an enclosed grassy path with a lake on your right. Bear left along a stony track, then leave the track and continue ahead along a narrow enclosed path. Go through woodland and continue through an adventure playground. Go down steps to Hale Oak Road.

For the shorter walk (and to considerably reduce stiles), turn left along this quiet road for about a mile and after the entrance to Hale Farm on your right, look for a footpath going left off a straight section of the road and turn left here. Pick up directions again at ** on page 158).

Turn right along the road for about 500 metres, and then turn left over a footbridge and stile just before a house and opposite a byway. Keep on the right side of the field and continue to a gate and stile. Go over the stile and a plank footbridge and continue straight downhill to a stream. Cross a stile and footbridge and then another stile into a field.

Go up and straight across, over a footbridge and then across another field. Go over a stile, cross a track and over another stile. Cross the next field on a left diagonal passing on the right side of a clump of trees and pond. Continue to the left side of a wood and go through a stile. Cross a track and go over a stile and footbridge ahead. Turn right and follow the edge of the wood to a field corner. Go over a stile and a footbridge and continue alongside the wood. Hale Oak Farm is on your left.

Join a paddock fence on your left and emerge into a large field. Bear left across the field towards a way-marked post next to a telegraph pole. Go through the gap in the fence and turn right along an enclosed grassy track. Turn left just before a gateway keeping the fence on your right. In about 20 metres turn right through a metal gate (concealed), cross a footbridge and then go up steps to a field corner. Go straight up across the field and pass a brick structure on your left, then veer left and then right along a track towards farm buildings and eventually reach the road (Bayleys Hill).

Turn left; pass the entrance to a house (Sharp's Place) and then go immediately left off the road up a bank and over a stile by a field gate. Pass an oast on your left and continue along a grassy track to another gate and go over a stile. Go along the left side of the field to the corner. Go through a kissing gate and continue along the left side to the next field corner. Go over a stile and follow an enclosed path between ponds. Pass a sand school on your right and soon come to a T junction.

Keep left, pass through a gate and continue through a narrow belt of wood. Continue to the end and emerge into a field. Go straight across passing on the right side of a pond concealed by trees. Continue to the edge and go through a gate into Hale Oak Road. Turn right and then immediately left along a footpath, going through a gateway.

** Go straight across the field passing Brownings Farm over on the right. Continue across the next field bearing right to the corner. Go through a gate into a wood and continue along a track. Emerge at a field corner and turn right going alongside the wood to another corner. Go directly ahead through a gap and cross the next field towards a kissing gate in the far left corner. Go through and continue along the left side of the field passing Charcott Farm on your left.

At the next corner go through a kissing gate and go slightly left across the field towards the left side of farm buildings, and between the first two telegraph poles. Go over the stile into the farm drive and turn left to the road. Turn left towards Charcott and over on the right you will see St. Lukes Church. Soon turn right to rejoin the tarmac footpath to Chiddingstone Causeway and Penshurst Station. At the road turn right and go downhill past the church to the station and 'The Little Brown Jug.'

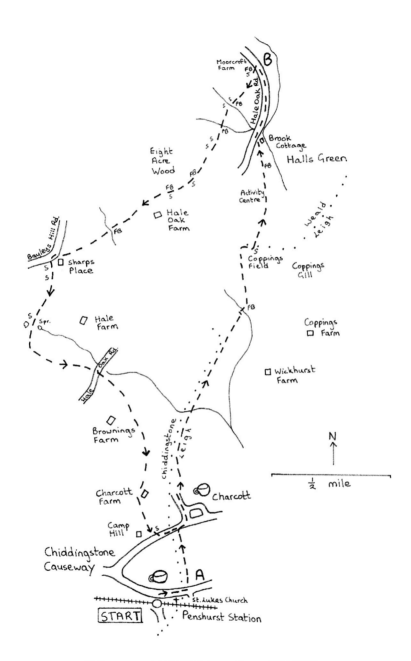

13 Weald and Fletchers Green

Maps:	OS Explorer 147
Distance:	2.5 miles
Stiles:	5 stiles
Start:	The Green; TQ 527508
Transport:	Bus 402; Weald/Tonbridge
Parking:	Memorial Village Hall
Refresh:	The Windmill Inn, Edwards Bar.

Weald is beautifully placed at the foot of the greensand ridge. It is an ideal place to start a gentle stroll which takes you through meadow, woods and green pastures lined with blossom filled hedges in spring. The views to the ridge and across the wealden countryside are fabulous.

'and so to the mead of Newsoles which is within..'

This walk will go through an area of meadowland between Weald and Nizels which is likely to be the 'mead of Newsoles,' especially as it is also the site of the old parish and hundred boundaries between Tonbridge and Sevenoaks (Codsheath hundred). Public footpaths follow the Tonbridge and Leigh boundary hedges for some distance. The jurors probably walked the same footpaths.

In about 1800, Hasted wrote of Weald that, "When a parish extends below (the greensand) and the church of it is above the hill, that part below has the addition of 'Weald' to it." Weald used to be part of Sevenoaks and in the parish of St. Nicholas. When St. Georges Church was built in 1821, for the first time, parishioners did not have to climb the hill to attend church.

Start

From the Memorial Village Hall car park on the Green, keep the hall on your right and continue along a tarmac path going downhill between houses to a road. Turn right, pass a private road and shortly go right again along a byway. Continue along this broad track through woodland until you come to a lane (Hale Oak Road). Turn left and look out on your left for a metal stile leading into a field.

Go through and straight across the field to a footbridge, cross over and climb steps up to a gate. Go through and cross the next field uphill, passing a telegraph pole and oak tree. Head for a way-marked gate, go through and cross the farm track to another gate. Go through and continue along the left side of the field to a kissing gate. Continue on the left side of the next field to another kissing gate. Go through passing a garden on your right to Scabharbour Road at Fletchers Green. Turn left and then right down Egg Pie Lane, looking out for a footpath on your left. Go over a stile and follow the right side of a long field passing a pond behind a post and rail fence. Aim for the far left corner and go over a stile. Turn right and follow a hedge on your right to a way-marked gate and stile in the hedge line, but don't go through.

161

The hedge on the other side of the gate is the old boundary of Tonbridge Parish. Just beyond is Nizels, a place recorded in the perambulation as 'Newsoles.'

With the boundary hedge on your right, keep straight on through a gateway, cross the field and go over a stile into the next field. Go straight across and over a stile where, behind the fence to the right, there is a boundary stone.

This stone marks the meeting of Tonbridge, Leigh and Weald (once Sevenoaks) Parishes. Such a significant place in the perambulation was probably recorded. This area is flat and criss-crossed with streams and therefore a strong contender for Newsoles (Nizels) mead (meadow).

Continue ahead with the hedge on your right. At the next corner, go over a stile and proceed along a track and through a kissing gate to Morleys Road. Turn left and soon after the pub (Edwards) turn right along a track

(by a large green sports ground sign). Continue along the track which becomes a footpath and at a T junction turn left, then fork left. Eventually come to a road (Glebe Road) and turn left, continuing to a crossroads. Turn right along Windmill Road and continue to the Village Green and Memorial Hall.

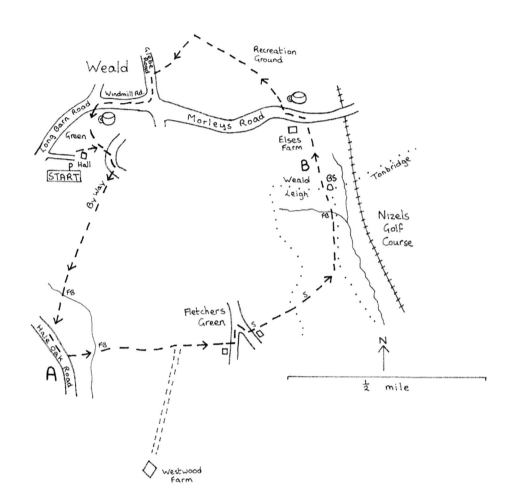

Weald

Windmill Rd.

Long Barn Road

Green

P Hall

START

By Way

Recreation Ground

Morleys Road

Elses Farm

B

Weald Leigh

BS

FB

Tonbridge

Nizels Golf Course

FB

S

FB

Fletchers Green

S

Hale Oak Road

A

FB

Westwood Farm

N

½ mile

163

14   Weald and Underriver

Maps:	OS Explorer 147
Distance:	6.5 miles
Stiles:	9 stiles
Start:	The Windmill; TQ 528509
Transport:	Bus 402; Weald/Tonbridge
Parking:	Weald Village
Refresh:	The Windmill, Weald
	The White Rock, Underriver

Weald is situated at the foot of the greensand ridge which marks the beginning of the vast region called 'the weald' extending southward to the South Downs. The perambulation and the lowy of Tonbridge are entirely within the weald. From here to the end of the walk at Shipbourne, the greensand ridge will make a dramatic backdrop to the tumbling pastures and bluebell coppiced woods of the weald.

'and so to the mead of Newsoles which is within..and so to the paved way and to Romdshedde..so the fee of the Earl is within..'

Newsoles is Nizels, famous now for golf. The 'paved way' must refer to the London Road which is an ancient route through Tonbridge and needs to be followed for a section of this walk. Romshed Farm still exists and is an old moat site with part in Sevenoaks and part in Tonbridge.

With 'The Windmill Inn' on your right, go along Windmill Road and then through the crossroads, continuing along Morleys Road. After Edwards Bar and Brasserie on your left and Elses Farm on your right, turn right and go through a kissing gate. Follow a track and keep straight on, soon going over a stile into a field. Go along the left side of the field to a stile and look for the boundary stone behind the fence on your left.

This stone is the meeting of the parishes of Tonbridge, Weald and Leigh. From this point you will be walking in the lowy of Tonbridge across meadow land which is likely to be the 'mead of Newsoles' (Nizels) recorded on the perambulation.

Go over the stile and bear left towards the railway line and field corner. Cross a footbridge and then veer left over another footbridge into the next field. Walk alongside the railway until you come to a tunnel going under on your left. Go over the stile and through the tunnel to emerge at Nizel's Golf Course. Go forward to a stony track and continue ahead, passing Hole 3 on your left. Keep straight on (leaving the track) and soon turn right over a footbridge by a way-marked post. Go uphill alongside a wood on your left and at the end, go directly across the golf course to a pond. Keep the pond on your left and go through a gate to Nizels Lane. Turn left along the lane passing Nizels Farm on your right and the entrance to the Golf Club on your left. Go across the road bridge over the A21 to London Road.

The original Nizels manor house was destroyed by fire in 1899. It was rebuilt, sold and opened as a Golf and Leisure Club in 1992.

The A21 Sevenoaks to Tonbridge By-Pass was opened by The Right Hon Edward Heath PM, in 1971. Local residents remember the problems caused by the wealden clay which walkers know plenty about. This section of the London Road (the paved way) was the first turnpike road in Kent to be opened in 1709.

Cross over the road and turn left. Pass Bank Lane on your right and the motel on your left and continue to Morley's roundabout.

Morleys is named after a farm of that name just by the road. The motel started life as Morley's farm hut selling teas and farm produce.

Pass St Julian's cottage on your right and just before St Julian's Lodge turn right along a restricted by-way. Go along this pleasant woodland path for about half a mile.

To the left is Riverhill which is a tautological name because the river comes from 'rither' (Old English hill), so the name means 'hill hill'.

St. Julians lodge is the beginning of a large estate once called Romdshedde Manor as in the perambulation. St Julians is a house on the estate, built in the 19th century, but Romshed Farm through which you will pass, still

preserves the old name. There is a story that a William Rumsched found a poor boy in Sevenoaks in the 14th century and adopted him, calling him William Sevenoke. He was later to become Lord Mayor of London and founder of Sevenoaks School.

Turn right through a kissing gate into Romshed Farm lands. Go along the left side of the field to the corner. Turn left to a gate with a stile.

This stile is on the Tonbridge/Sevenoaks boundary and an older version of it was crossed by the jurors on the perambulation. The boundary continues ahead through the farm buildings where perhaps they rested for awhile.

Go over the stile and cross the field towards the right side of the farm buildings. At the corner go over a stile, cross the farm drive and over another stile. Turn left across the field towards a pond and a field gate.

The pond is near the site of an old moat which was probably the site of the farmhouse in the 13th century. The perambulation route came through the middle of Romshed manor (spelt in many different ways; sometimes Rumshott) as the parish and constituency boundary does today.

Cross the stile and go directly ahead to another gate and go over the stile (now leaving the Tonbridge boundary). Go straight on uphill across the field passing left of a telegraph pole. At a gate, go through and follow an enclosed path. Soon turn right following the fence round and go through an area of woodland to a recreation ground. Keep along the right side to the corner and go over a stile to the road (Carters Hill) at Underriver. Turn left and continue up Carters Hill, passing the White Rock Inn on your right.

Underriver means 'under the hill' and certainly the greensand ridge dominates the village so that it looks almost 'alpine'.The beauty of the area drew artists such as Samuel Palmer (1805-1881) who painted and sketched a number of landscapes from the top of the hill or lower down in the vicinity of the village.

Local residents have written a book on his work entitled, 'Underriver; Samuel Palmer's Golden Valley' by Griselda Barton with Michael Tong.

Continue to a crossroads and turn left along the bridleway passing Kettleshill Cottage on your right. Go between two white painted fence sections, pass Black Charles on your right with its ragstone wall and continue uphill along the footpath.

Ragstone is the local building stone found in the hills here and it is a common material in Sevenoaks houses and walls. Old houses such as Black Charles were built near springs issuing from the lower slopes of the greensand ridge. There is a reference to a John Blakecherl (meaning dark man) in the 14th century. Black Charles was probably his house.

Arrive at a path junction and go straight on to a paved lane passing the unusual stone oasts of Kettleshill Farm on your right and on your left Kettleshill House and then farm buildings. Continue uphill, now on a stony track passing a house at the top. Go downhill past The Coach House on your right, then turn left along a restricted by-way. Pass a lake on your right from where you can see St. Julians house.

Now a private members' club, it was built in the early 19th century by the Herries family who owned the estate of Romshed Manor.

Continue along the by-way and you will eventually see Romshed Farm over on the left. Pass through a wood and at the end you will see the gate to the farm through which you passed earlier. Continue back to Weald by retracing your steps.

If you need reminding of the way, continue to the London Road at Morley's roundabout and turn left along the pavement passing Bank Lane. Turn next right along Nizels Lane. Go over the A21 and continue, passing the Golf and Country Club entrance. When the lane bears left, turn right at the first footpath sign and pass a pond on your right. Go across the golf course and keep alongside the wood downhill to a footbridge. Cross over and turn left passing Hole 3 on your right. Continue through a tunnel under the railway and go over a stile into a field.

Turn right and follow the railway line to nearly the end of the field, then bear left to the field corner. Cross a footbridge and then veer right to go over another footbridge. Bear left and soon reach the stile in the next hedge by the boundary stone. Go over the stile and continue with the hedge on your right to the next corner. Cross a stile and continue along a track, go through a gate and into Morleys Road, turn left and continue through crossroads to 'The Windmill Inn' by the Green.

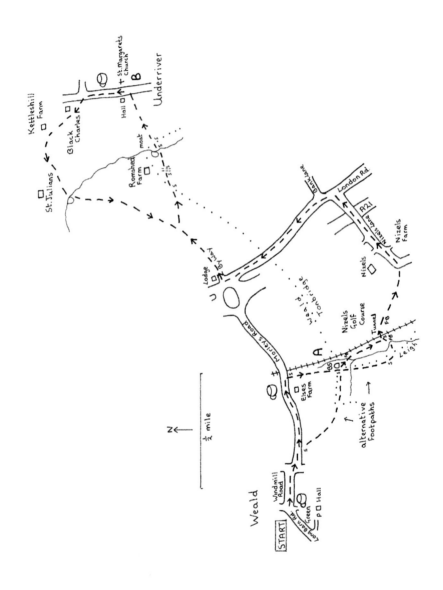

Underriver and Shipbourne

Maps:	OS Explorer 147
Distance:	5.5 miles
Stiles:	28 stiles
Start:	St Margarets Church;
	TQ 556520
Parking:	Underriver
Refresh:	The White Rock, Underriver
	The Chaser Inn, Shipbourne

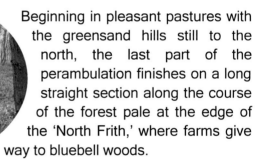

Beginning in pleasant pastures with the greensand hills still to the north, the last part of the perambulation finishes on a long straight section along the course of the forest pale at the edge of the 'North Frith,' where farms give way to bluebell woods.

'so the fee of the Earl is within and Holindenne without..and so directly to the pale of the forest so the tenements of the Earl are always within..and so by the pale of the forest to Somegate..'

Between Underriver and Hildenborough there is a large area called Hollanden which was outside the lowy. The perambulation diverted south from Underriver, visiting places in Hollanden to confirm the boundaries. Individual locations are elusive but Hollanden is marked on old OS maps. From Hollanden the walk joins the old forest pale of the North Frith, the Clares' hunting forest.

Start

From the church gate in Underriver, pass the church on your left and then turn left along a restricted by-way. Pass houses on your left and continue straight on through a kissing gate into a field and go along the left side and through into the next field. Veer left through a line of oak trees to the left  corner and go over a stile. Continue along the left side of the next field through an avenue of oaks and go through a gate, then over a stile and through another gate. Continue along the left side of the field to the next corner. Go over a stile to a road (Underriver House Road).

The by-way was clearly once a wide lane or drove and is a direct route between Shipbourne and Underriver.

Turn right and follow the road for about a quarter of a mile then turn left over a stile just before a house called Hollandhurst. Bear left across the field towards a stile in the next hedge. Go over and bear right across the field keeping near to the right hedge and continuing towards the right side of a row of houses. Join a paddock fence on your right; shortly turn right over a stile and cross the paddock to another stile. Cross over the stile and a footbridge and then turn left along the track passing Grenadier cottages. Continue to Riding Lane.

The houses are named after a pub called 'The Grenadier' which is marked on late 19th century maps but was flattened by a bomb in 1942. They are just within the district called Hollanden and the Tonbridge forest, the North Frith begins on the other side of Riding Lane.

Turn right and continue along Riding Lane passing Gardener's Hope cottages on your right. After a short while turn left at a footpath sign onto a tarmac drive to Fairhill. Go across a bridge and follow the drive between laurel hedges passing the entrance to Fairhill. As the drive bears left continue ahead, over a stile and then uphill through bluebell woods. At the end of the wood, go over a stile and along an enclosed path next to a field.

Notice the bank and mature hedge on your left as you walk. The 13th century forest pale and the Tonbridge boundary followed (and still does) the left side of the footpath. You are walking as the jurors did, 'and so by the pale of the forest'

Go over the next stile, cross a track and then a bridge to a green metal gate. Cross the stile and continue along an enclosed path to another stile. Go over and continue through a wood where the footpath will go over the boundary bank. Come out of the wood to a field and continue alongside the left hedge. Tinley Lodge Farm is over on the right. Go through a gate and continue straight ahead to a farm drive.

Turn left, pass a new house on your right and then turn right through a wood. Continue along an enclosed path with a tall deer fence on your right.

Eventually bear right round a cypressus hedge, cross a drive and instead of going straight on, veer left in front of a wooden field gate and follow an enclosed path between fields to a hedge. Go through the hedge to Hildenborough Road. Cross over and turn right along a wide grass verge.

This is West Green where Hasted places 'Somegate;' the start and finish of the perambulation.

Shortly turn left along a footpath, cross a footbridge and go directly across a field to a yellow painted post at the corner of a wood. Continue alongside the wood on your left to the corner and then keep ahead across the field and at a stream, turn right towards the church. Aim for a yellow post at the other side of the field and turn left following the hedge on your right. Come to a small stand of trees and at the field corner turn right through a kissing gate into the church yard. Follow the church round and continue to the lych gate to emerge on Stumble Hill at Shipbourne and the end of the perambulation!

St Giles Church in Shipbourne was built in 1879 by Edward Cazalet of Fairlawn although there has been a church on the site since mediaeval times. Constructed of ragstone, the lichen has given it an interesting red hue. The Chaser Inn is next door to the church.

To return to Underriver, go back through the churchyard and through the kissing gate and go straight on across the field with a hedge on your right. Continue uphill towards the corner of a wood, following yellow posts and go over a stile into the wood. Continue on a wide path through the wood and at a path junction, turn left and go uphill. Keep on the path in roughly the same direction and eventually emerge at Budds Green on Mote Road.

Turn left and then towards the end of a small Green, turn right along a restricted by-way alongside the drive of Great Budds. Go along an enclosed path passing a barn on your left and follow the path as it turns in front of a pond. Keep the pond on your left and go over a stile. Go straight across a field along a stony track and through the next field in the same direction.

Go over a footbridge and then a stile and then another stile by a field gate. Keep straight ahead along the right fence towards a barn. At the field corner, go over a stile and pass through a yard with the barn on your right. Go over two stiles into the next field. Keep to the right side of the field alongside a wood towards Underriver House.

At the next corner go over a stile and turn right alongside a stream. Continue straight ahead to a wooden gate and turn left round the back of a hedge and keep to the left of a drive. Soon join the drive and pass houses until you come to the road (Underriver House Road). Turn left and pass a pond on your right and then Underriver House on your left.

Underriver House used to be the manor of Shoads; the name was changed when the house was rebuilt in the 18th century.

Turn right along a footpath opposite the house; go over a stile and cross a footbridge into a field. Cross the field directly ahead and then go through a gateway or over a stile and keeping the small wood on your left, go up across the field towards an oak tree. Keep it on your left, go over a stile and continue across the next field. Cross a stile and go across the next field.

Go over another stile and cross the next field heading to the right of poplar trees. Cross another stile and continue to the double line of poplars ahead. Keep the poplars on your left and go alongside to a stile in the field corner. Follow a short enclosed path to a stile and emerge on Carters Hill at Underriver. Turn left for the 'White Rock' pub and centre of the village.

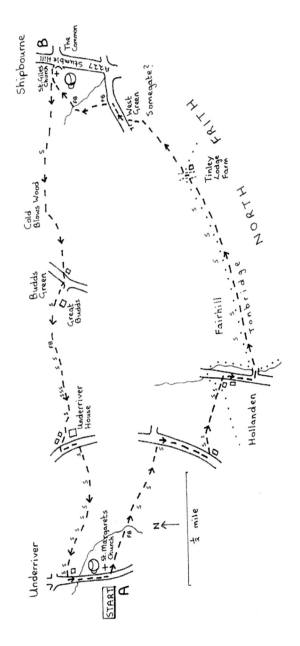

176